IMAGES
of America

SPRING GROVE
STATE HOSPITAL

SPRING GROVE BICENTENNIAL COVERLET. This coverlet was created in celebration of Spring Grove's bicentennial in 1997. It is currently on display in the Spring Grove Alumni Museum.

IMAGES
of America

SPRING GROVE
STATE HOSPITAL

David S. Helsel, M.D.,
and Trevor J. Blank

ARCADIA
PUBLISHING

Published by Arcadia Publishing
Charleston SC, Chicago IL, Portsmouth NH, San Francisco CA

Library of Congress Catalog Card Number: 2007937955

For all general information contact Arcadia Publishing at:
Telephone 843-853-2070
Fax 843-853-0044
E-mail sales@arcadiapublishing.com
For customer service and orders:
Toll-Free 1-888-313-2665

Visit us on the Internet at www.arcadiapublishing.com

*To the patients and staff of Spring Grove Hospital Center,
past and present.*

CONTENTS

ACKNOWLEDGMENTS

The authors would like to thank the citizens of the state of Maryland (Martin O'Malley, governor). Maryland serves as a leader in the provision of publicly funded mental health services. The authors gratefully acknowledge the support of Spring Grove Hospital Center by the Maryland Department of Health and Mental Hygiene (John M. Colmers, secretary); and the Maryland Mental Hygiene Administration (Brian Hepburn, M.D., executive director). The authors wish to express deep appreciation to the patients and staff of Spring Grove Hospital Center, past and present. In particular, we wish to thank Spring Grove staff members Juanita White, Theresa Gordon, Evette Jones, and David Lembeck. Dr. David Helsel would like to thank his parents, Dale and Doris Helsel, for passing down their keen interest in history, tradition, and storytelling. The authors are indebted to the Spring Grove Alumni Museum volunteers, all of whom have worked tirelessly over the years to record, preserve, and share the hospital's rich history. Additional thanks go to Robert W. Schoeberlein, director of Special Collections for the Maryland State Archives. Both Rob and the Maryland State Archives in Annapolis have served as invaluable resources in the preparation of this book. The authors wish to acknowledge the Baltimore County Public Library, the Baltimore County Historical Society, the University of Maryland, and the Maryland Historical Society.

Trevor Blank would like to thank his wife, Rebecca, who not only diligently critiqued and refined his writing style, but who also provided immeasurable moral support throughout the book's production. Special thanks are due to his parents, Bruce and Anita, for their support. The helpful and attentive staff at the University of Maryland's Special Collections, especially Jennie Levine, was instrumental in obtaining several images for the book. The members of the Hillcrest Historical Society—Michael Abrams, Charles Kucera, Berchie Manley, Wayne Smith, and David Wasmund—have shared enthusiasm for historic preservation and community involvement. Trevor's friends at the University of Maryland, Baltimore County—Warren Belasco, Kathy Bryan, Jason Loviglio, and Ed Orser—and his colleagues at Indiana University—Henry Glassie, Jason Jackson, John McDowell, and Pravina Shukla—have been invaluable throughout the book's production for their friendship and support. Lastly, Maryland folklorist Charley Camp supplied Trevor with Old Bay Seasoning and sage advice while he pursued a graduate degree at Indiana University's Folklore Institute—a far distance from the Old Line State.

Unless otherwise noted, all images herein are courtesy of the archives at Spring Grove Hospital Center, Catonsville, Maryland.

All of the book's royalties will go to benefit the Spring Grove Patient Welfare Fund.

INTRODUCTION

Several years ago, a patient of Spring Grove State Hospital jokingly suggested that the motto of the hospital ought to be: "Spring Grove: Where out of mind is out of sight." The double entendre and the possibly stigmatizing element of that statement aside, the fact remains that state hospitals such as Spring Grove often have been out of sight, mysterious, and unfamiliar to the majority of us.

Of course, our views of state psychiatric hospitals have largely to do with the degree to which our society has traditionally been uncomfortable with the entire subject of mental illness. The subject of state psychiatric hospitals, not unlike that of mental illness itself, has been one that is for some people more comfortably considered in broad or stereotypic terms. And so it is not surprising that our culture has tended to mystify and even stigmatize state hospitals. Opinions about places such as Spring Grove are undoubtedly shaped not so much by personal experience, but by the many depictions of state psychiatric hospitals that exist in our culture: in literature, in movies, on television, in jokes, and in folklore. These often contradictory depictions are typically broadly painted and a bit simplistic. Sometimes the images with which we are presented in popular culture are comedic, and sometimes the images are more touching, painful, or poignant. In some instances, state hospitals are shown as places of recovery, hope, triumph, or inspiration. And sometimes they are portrayed as being disturbing, frightening, or even sinister.

But while our mental images of state hospitals may be largely shaped by the confluence of the various depictions of them that stem from our popular culture, and while discomfort with the subject of mental illness may also mitigate, our ideas about state hospitals clearly also have something to do with the very nature of the hospitals themselves—at least as they were originally conceived. At one time, state hospitals were called "asylums," and as such, they were intentionally built in fairly remote settings so that they could provide private, protected, and intentionally insulated surroundings for the mentally ill. As a result, state hospitals tended to became worlds unto themselves—places that were remote, mysterious, locked, and hidden behind iron gates. They were, indeed, quite literally out of sight, and therefore, they were places that could only be imagined by most.

And therein lies the problem with any brief book about the history of a state psychiatric hospital: state hospitals have been imagined and stereotyped to the degree that many people have largely inaccurate yet sometimes rigidly fixed ideas about them. Within this context, the authors are aware that in the publication of a book of this nature, they run the risk of over-simplification of the subject matter or of inadvertently perpetuating some of the stereotypic ideas that people may have of psychiatric patients and psychiatric hospitals such as Spring Grove.

In these few pages, and bound by the limitations of the often idealized historic images that are available to us, it will be impossible to accurately depict and fully explain an institution as complex as Spring Grove State Hospital. The fact is that Spring Grove is a very large and very old state hospital that has existed to serve a single purpose for over 200 years. As one would expect of any such institution, the hospital is rich in tradition. There are also amazing stories, idiosyncrasies, contradictions, and, sometimes, baffling levels of complexity. The reality is that Spring Grove has always provided a safety net for Maryland's citizens, and it is truly a place of hope, healing, recovery, courage, compassion, and triumph. But, at the same time, it is also a place that holds a great deal of unhappiness and human suffering. It must be remembered, therefore, that the images in this book are intended only to provide a brief impression of a historic hospital, and not a comprehensive consideration of the hospital's history or its traditions. Our hope is simply that through the images in this book we can dispel some of the historically negative images of state hospitals and their patients.

Spring Grove State Hospital, with its long and rich history, serves not only as an excellent example of historic institutions of its kind, but also as an embodiment of the history of American public inpatient mental health treatment. It was founded in 1797 and, with certain caveats, can claim to be the second-oldest continuously operating psychiatric hospital in the United States. Only the Eastern State Hospital in Williamsburg, Virginia, is older. Spring Grove was established by the State of Maryland at a time when yellow fever was a top public health concern in Baltimore and the predominant model for the care of the mentally ill was largely one of confinement. In the 19th century, Spring Grove adopted the principles of moral therapy, a model that promoted recovery through structure, occupation, fresh air, and a healthy lifestyle. In the 20th century, Spring Grove continued to apply the tenets of moral therapy but also adopted employed psychoanalytic techniques and, later, biological psychiatry.

Students of the history of Spring Grove are sometimes confused by the fact that the hospital has had so many different names over the years. It was originally called the Public Hospital of Baltimore. Other official and unofficial names have included the Baltimore Hospital, the City Hospital, the Hospital in the Vicinity of Baltimore, the Maryland Hospital, the Maryland Hospital for the Insane at Baltimore, the Maryland Hospital for the Insane at Spring Grove, the Spring Grove Asylum, and the Spring Grove State Hospital. It is currently known as Spring Grove Hospital Center. Further complicating the hospital's nomenclature is the fact that it had a limited-service predecessor institution, founded three years earlier in 1794, at the same location. That institution has been variously referred to as the Retreat, the Hospital for Strangers and Mariners, the Hospital for Seamen and Strangers, and the Retreat for Strangers and Mariners. For the sake of simplicity, the authors have often chosen to refer to the hospital as "Spring Grove" or "Spring Grove State Hospital," even when the reference is to the hospital at time during which it was operating under a different name. Yet another potential source of confusion is the fact that the hospital that is known today as Spring Grove was originally located in Baltimore and operated there until 1872, when it was relocated to its present site in Catonsville, Maryland.

We truly hope that you enjoy this look at what we think is a fascinating and truly remarkable institution. For further information, please visit the Spring Grove Web site at www.springgrove. com or the Spring Grove Alumni Museum, which is located in the Garrett Building on the grounds of Spring Grove.

One

THE BALTIMORE YEARS
1797–1871

During the first 75 years of its history, Spring Grove State Hospital was located in the city of Baltimore, near Broadway on a parcel of land that is now occupied by the Johns Hopkins Hospital. Founded in 1797, the institution did not relocate to its present-day site in Catonsville until 1872. Although Spring Grove has operated under a number of different names over the years, it has always been a state-owned hospital operated under the authority of the State of Maryland.

The hospital initially was chartered by the Maryland General Assembly to serve as both an asylum for the mentally ill and as a general hospital for persons with non-psychiatric illnesses. In 1814, during the War of 1812, some 234 sick and wounded soldiers were taken to the hospital that would become known as Spring Grove State Hospital from the battles that occurred around Baltimore, including the Battle of North Point. Yellow fever patients were treated at the hospital during several epidemics that occurred in the Baltimore area between 1798 and 1819. Spring Grove always served as a safety net for those who required care and treatment but who were unable to pay for it. In the beginning, the annual fee for public patients was $100 per patient. Private patients typically paid between $3 and $5 a week, or $150 and $260 per year.

The percentage of non-psychiatric patients at the hospital declined over the years, and by the 1830s, all patients admitted to the institution had mental illnesses. The hospital's early records report that certain patients were permitted the freedom "to go partially at large," and it was further noted the hospital maintained horses and carriages so patients could leave the grounds for long carriage rides and other activities. However, many, or perhaps most, patients were kept in "strict confinement"—either in individual rooms, which were called "cells," or behind the hospital's high walls. Female patients were engaged in sewing, laundry, and gardening. Male patients worked on the hospital's eight-acre farm or performed other tasks, such as carpentry.

Despite a number of shortcomings, the hospital was considered to be one of the leading psychiatric institutions in the United States. Perhaps in recognition of that fact, the fifth meeting of what was to become the American Psychiatric Association was held at the original Spring Grove State Hospital in 1856.

EARLIEST KNOWN IMAGE OF THE HOSPITAL, 1801. This image is taken from an 1801 map of Baltimore. The original building was situated near where the domed administration building of the Johns Hopkins Hospital stands today. Spring Grove's limited-service predecessor institution, the Retreat for Seamen and Strangers was founded in 1794 and is believed to have stood at approximately the same site. It evidently was abandoned when the Public Hospital of Baltimore (later known as Spring Grove) was built.

THE ORIGINAL SPRING GROVE STATE HOSPITAL. The original c. 1798 building eventually became the westernmost section of a largely expanded hospital building. This cropped image, taken from a lithograph of the completed hospital, gives the viewer an idea of the appearance of the original building.

MAP OF BALTIMORE, 1801. This detail of a Baltimore map shows the approximate location of the hospital in 1801. The crossroads were a now abandoned byway known as the "Old Road to Philadelphia" (near today's Monument Street) and Market Street (now known as Broadway). Fells Point was to the hospital's south. The original six-and-three-quarter-acre grounds were reportedly purchased by the state of Maryland from a sea captain, Jeremiah Yellott, in 1798 at a cost of £800. Eventually the landholdings were expanded to approximately 13 acres and included an eight-acre farm. (Courtesy of Baltimore County Historical Society.)

THE HOSPITAL IN HOSPITAL SQUARE, 1819. The cross streets, as shown in this image, were Market (later Broadway) and Jefferson Streets. The location of the hospital and what was called "Hospital Square" is spotted on this map to the immediate right of the "E" in "Baltimore." (Courtesy of Baltimore County Historical Society.)

LETTER FROM THE ORIGINAL SPRING GROVE STATE HOSPITAL DURING THE WAR OF 1812. The letter reads: "Gentlemen, There are in the Hospital at this time about thirty sick and wounded soldiers, many of whom are altogether destitute of bedding. They also stand in need of a daily supply of fresh beef and flour. The committee will please to take the subject into consideration, and adopt some mode by which these necessary articles may be supplied. Very respectfully, Colin MacKenzie." The petitioner, Dr. MacKenzie, was one of the two physicians who were in charge of the hospital at the time. The letter is dated on the day before the Battle of North Point.

THE ORIGINAL SPRING GROVE STATE HOSPITAL IN 1816. This rather fuzzy image of Spring Grove appeared as an illustration on an 1816 map of the city of Baltimore. In 1816, Spring Grove was known as the Baltimore Hospital. (Courtesy of Baltimore County Historical Society.)

BALTIMORE GROWS. The location of the hospital is indicated by the arrow in the upper right corner of this 1836 map of eastern Baltimore. (Courtesy of Baltimore County Historical Society.)

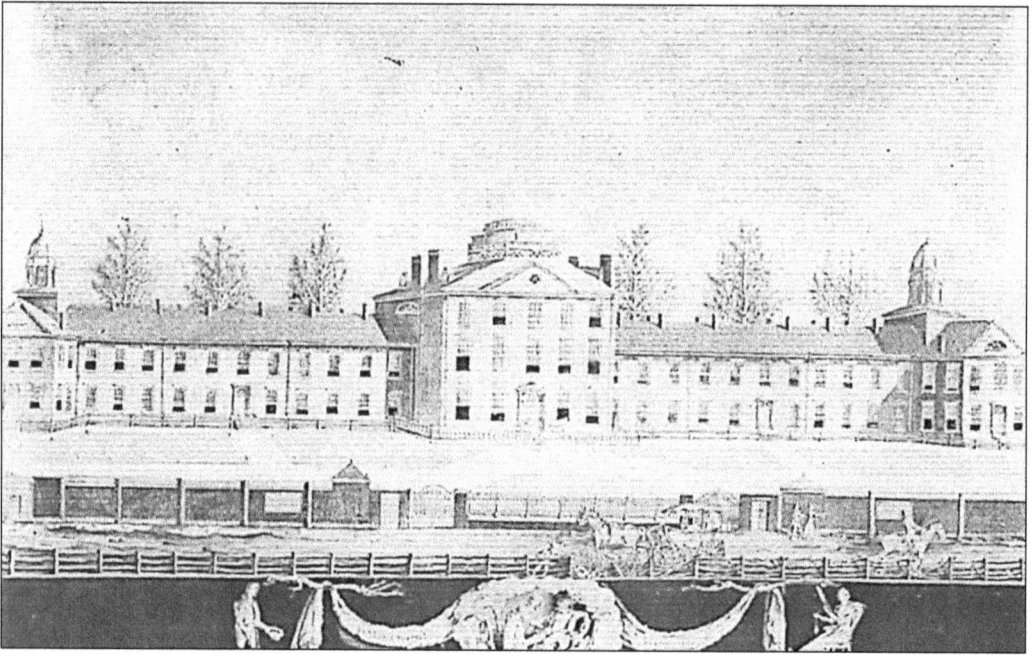

THE COMPLETED HOSPITAL IN ITS BALTIMORE LOCATION. This image shows the appearance of the hospital in the 1830s following its completion. The original building can be seen as the structure at the far right side of the image. (Courtesy of Maryland State Archives.)

JOHNS HOPKINS. Johns Hopkins's affiliation with Spring Grove began in 1852 when he was elected as a member of the hospital's board of visitors. Hopkins eventually purchased the still-occupied Maryland Hospital property from the state in 1870, with the intent to build his own hospital at the site. He generously agreed to pay for the property in advance of his taking actual possession of it—a circumstance that allowed the hospital to continue to operate in its old quarters until the new hospital at the Spring Grove site could be completed. The infusion of cash from the sale of the old hospital allowed the state to complete the new hospital building at Spring Grove in October 1872. Hopkins never lived to see the hospital that bears his name, which was built at the original site of Spring Grove. He died on Christmas Eve 1873. (Courtesy of Johns Hopkins Medical Institutions.)

SPRING GROVE RECORD FROM 1817. The document reads: "This is to certify that Mr. Benjamin Sewell was restored to perfect health of body and mind in the course of two weeks after his admission into the Balt[imore] Hospital, and has continued well to this time." It was signed by the two physicians who operated the hospital in the early 1800s, Drs. Colin Mackenzie and James Smyth. The Baltimore Hospital was Spring Grove State Hospital's name in 1817. (Courtesy of Maryland State Archives.)

EARLY VIEW OF THE SPRING GROVE STATE HOSPITAL IN ITS BALTIMORE LOCATION. This view shows the nearly completed hospital in its original location in Baltimore, sometime around 1819. (Courtesy of Maryland Historical Society.)

15

ILLUSTRATION FROM 1822. This depiction of the "Hospital in the Vicinity of Baltimore" is an illustration found on an 1822 map of Baltimore. The caption above the picture reads: "Hospital—In Hospital Square. Built by Balt[imore] County." The bottom portion of the picture notes that the hospital was "Enlarged by Donations from the State of Maryland [and] cost $140,000" as of 1822. (Courtesy of Baltimore County Historical Society.)

OVERLAY MAP OF THE VICINITY OF THE HOSPITAL, 1850. This map shows the location of the hospital and some of its then-present outbuildings, superimposed over markings that indicated the location of earlier structures. The Carnegie Building of Johns Hopkins Hospital now stands at the approximate location of the Superintendent's House.

16

TABLE IV.
Ages of Patients in the House during the year.

From 20 to 25,	16	Brought forward,	121
25 to 30,	25	From 50 to 55,	9
30 to 35,	36	55 to 60,	6
35 to 40,	14	60 to 65,	2
40 to 45,	17	65 to 70,	1
45 to 50,	13	70 to 75,	2
		Over 75,	1
	121		142

TABLE V.
Supposed causes of Disease in the cases under treatment during the year.

Intemperance,	26
Ill health,	18
Masturbation,	10
Constitutional,	7
Domestic trouble,	7
Religious excitement,	6
Pecuniary losses,	6
Want of employment,	5
Puerperal,	4
Disappointed affection,	3
Use of tobacco,	3
Intense study,	2
Political excitement,	1
Remorse,	1
Unknown,	43
	142

TABLE VI.
Forms of Insanity.

There were of Mania,	59
" Monomania,	36
" Dementia,	45
" Idiocy,	2
	142

TABLE VII.
Causes of Death.

Pulmonary Consumption,	2
Chronic Diarrhœa,	2
General Paralysis,	1
Chronic Disease of the Liver,	1
Cerebral Congestion,	1
Marasmus,	1
	8

TABLE VIII.
Residence of the Patients in the House during the year.

Maryland,	103
District of Columbia,	20
Virginia,	10
Pennsylvania,	5
Alabama,	2
North Carolina,	1
Connecticut,	1
There were of private Patients,	92
At public charge,	50
	142

TABLE IX.
Of the inmates at public charge, there were

		Brought forward,	18
From Talbot County,	3	From Howard District,	1
Queen Anne's County,	2	Carrol County,	1
Kent County,	1	Prince George's County,	1
Caroline County,	1	Charles County,	1
Dorchester County,	1	Calvert County,	1
Cecil County,	1	St. Mary's County,	2
Harford County,	2		25
Montgomery County,	3		
Frederick County,	2	City of Baltimore,	9
Anne Arundel County,	2	District of Columbia,	16
	18		50

There were in the House, 7 coloured patients:
Of whom 4 were free and 3 slaves.

ANNUAL REPORT OF THE RESIDENT PHYSICIAN, 1842. These two pages, photographed from the original, include demographic information about the patients under care in that year. Note the entry in the lower right corner, which reads: "There were in the House, 7 coloured [*sic*] patients: Of whom 4 were free and 3 slaves."

BALTIMORE PHILANTHROPIST ENOCH PRATT. Enoch Pratt was elected to the board of visitors of the Maryland Hospital (Spring Grove) in 1857 and remained actively involved in the hospital's affairs for several decades. Always a generous donor to Spring Grove, Pratt had stipulated in his will that, upon his death, a sizable portion of his estate was to be used to complete construction of the Sheppard Asylum in Towson, Maryland. Pratt died in 1896, and the Sheppard Asylum was eventually renamed the Sheppard and Enoch Pratt Hospital in his memory.

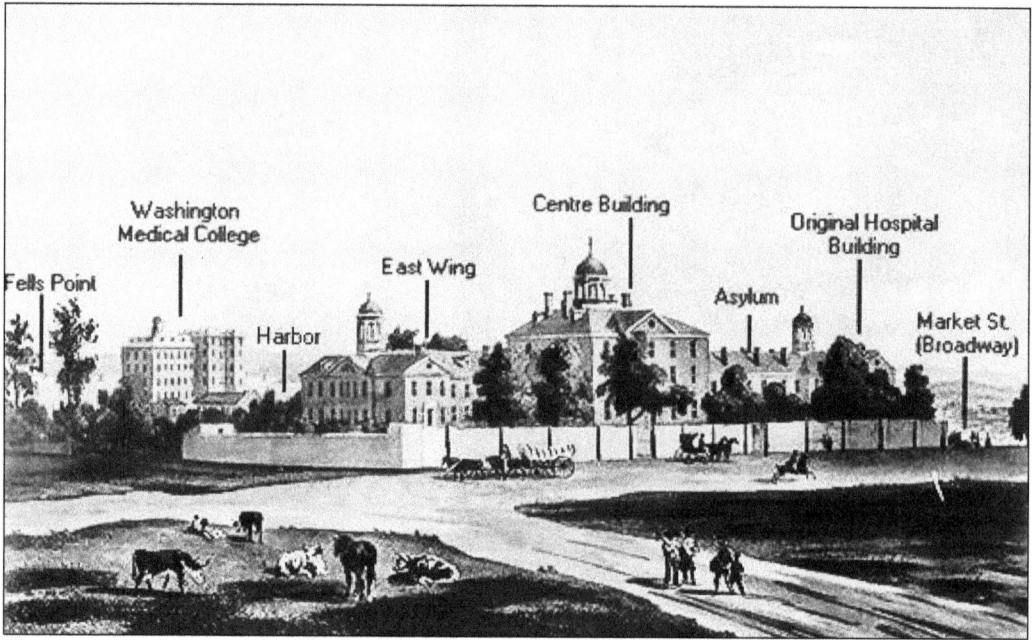

THE MARYLAND HOSPITAL, 1840s. This lithograph shows Spring Grove in its original location in Baltimore City. The tall building in the left background was the Washington Medical College and Hospital, later the Church Hospital. The Washington College Building is still extant. A historic footnote is that the poet Edgar Allan Poe died at the Washington College Hospital in 1849.

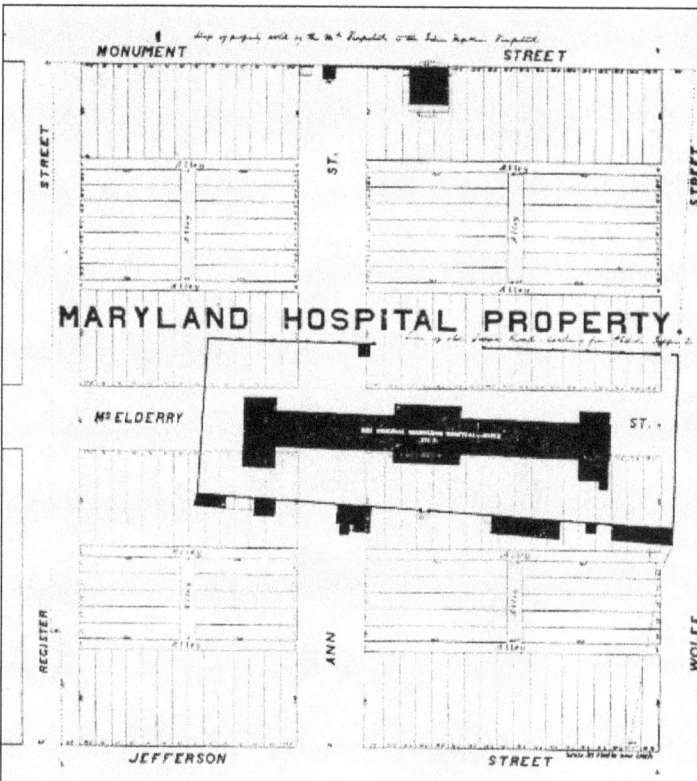

PROPOSAL TO SUBDIVIDE THE SITE OF THE ORIGINAL HOSPITAL IN BALTIMORE. The through-streets and building lots that are shown in this drawing never actually existed. Instead it was prepared in or around 1868 as part of an effort to establish the potential pecuniary value of the property in anticipation of its being put on the market for sale.

Dr. Richard Sprigg Steuart. As president of the hospital's board of visitors, Dr. Richard Sprigg Steuart chaired the committee that selected the hospital's current site at Spring Grove in Catonsville in 1852. An interesting footnote is that Dr. Steuart was relieved of his duties as president of the board of visitors during the Civil War when, in 1864, he refused to sign an oath of loyalty to the Union. He was reinstated in 1868. Evidently quite a character, Steuart lost his job again in 1875 when the board, under his leadership, mortgaged Spring Grove to private creditors and risked foreclosure after the Maryland Legislature refused to fully fund its operations.

Dr. Richard Sprigg Steuart
Painted by M. Louisa Steuart

Dorothea Lynde Dix (April 4, 1802–July 17, 1887). In 1852, in an impassioned plea before the Maryland General Assembly, Dorothea Dix, the outspoken advocate and crusader for the mentally ill, pointed to the various inadequacies of the Maryland Hospital for the Insane—chief among them its urban setting. She emphasized the need to relocate the hospital to more pastoral, rural surroundings. Dix's lobbying efforts are given much of the credit for the decision of the Maryland Legislature to fund the construction of the new hospital building at Spring Grove in Catonsville.

ARCHITECT'S ORIGINAL DESIGN FOR THE NEW HOSPITAL. The new hospital at Spring Grove was designed in 1853 by a noted Baltimore architect, J. Crawford Neilson (1816–1900). Neilson also designed the South Carolina State House and was one of the founders of the Baltimore chapter of the American Institute of Architects.

BALTIMORE HOSPITAL RAZED TO MAKE ROOM FOR JOHNS HOPKINS HOSPITAL, C. 1873. When this photograph was taken, all that remained of the original hospital was the wall that had once surrounded it. Patients and staff had moved from the original Baltimore location of the hospital to Spring Grove's present-day site in Catonsville in 1872.

Two

EARLY DAYS AT THE SPRING GROVE SITE
1872–1919

In late 1852, a 136-acre parcel in Catonsville was selected as the site for the new hospital. The property overlooked the city of Baltimore and was known as Spring Grove because it contained a number of spring-fed ponds and streams.

By the end of November 1852, the noted Maryland architect J. Crawford Neilson was selected to design the new hospital. Construction of the new building began in 1853. Because of funding shortfalls, construction progressed very slowly—and was stopped entirely by the onset of the Civil War in 1861. Major construction did not resume until 1870. The new hospital at the Spring Grove was designed to serve 325 patients and officially opened on October 7, 1872, when 112 patients of the old hospital in Baltimore were transferred there. The hospital's name was subsequently changed from the Maryland Hospital for the Insane at Baltimore to the Maryland Hospital for the Insane at Spring Grove.

The period from 1872 to 1920 might be referred to as Spring Grove's golden age. Staff and patients lived side-by-side, worked together on the farm and in the shops, and together were able to share the pleasures of the bucolic surroundings. Also during this period, Spring Grove grew and prospered as one of the leading state hospitals in America. As testimony to this, the American Medico Psychological Association, forerunner of the American Psychiatric Association, held its annual meeting in Baltimore in honor of Spring Grove's centennial in 1897.

The primary modality used to treat mental illness at the time was called "moral therapy." A variant of the Protestant work ethic, the tenets of moral therapy held that seriously ill psychiatric patients would improve and recover when provided structure, dignity, security, a pastoral living environment, social outlets, outdoor work, opportunities for regular exercise, fresh air, wholesome food, spiritual guidance, and clean, orderly surroundings. Accordingly, hospital authorities encouraged patients to spend time enjoying the fresh air and park-like setting of the hospital grounds. Fresh food from the farm was regularly available, there was steady work for all patients who were able, and activities were provided throughout the year.

LITHOGRAPH BY A. HOEN AND COMPANY, 1882. This rather idealized rendering of Spring Grove's Main Building shows elegantly dressed couples strolling through the hospital's grounds, while a horse-drawn carriage arrives at the carriage porch and another carriage makes its way up the drive. By the start of the Civil War, the entire north wing (right side of the above image) and the first two floors of the center section had been substantially finished. Several histories of the hospital report that the then-unoccupied north wing of the hospital was used to quarter Union troops or to care for wounded soldiers during the Civil War, but this has not been confirmed. The Main Building was built of stone that had been quarried on-site at Spring Grove.

MAIN BUILDING'S ORIGINAL FLOOR PLAN. The above plan of the new hospital at Spring Grove was published in the hospital's annual report of 1872–1873. The layout is typical of the so-called Kirkbride Plan buildings of the era in that it consists of a series of wings emanating *en echelon* from a monumental center building. As the floor plan indicates, male and female patients were housed on opposite sides of the building. Healthier convalescent patients were placed on the wards located closest to the entrance, while the more behaviorally disturbed patients occupied what later became known as the "back wards." The staggered arrangement also allowed for greater privacy and for most rooms to have exterior walls so that there would be lots of sunlight and fresh air. The Kirkbride building plan was promoted by the Philadelphia physician Thomas Story Kirkbride, and between 1845 and 1906, approximately 60 Kirkbride Plan hospitals were built in the United States. Heat was piped into the building from a boiler house located in a separate structure behind the hospital. The boiler house doubled as a gas works where gas for lighting was made from coal, and from the beginning, the building was illuminated at night by gaslights. Although the Main Building was torn down in 1964, the original *c.* 1853 boiler house is still standing as the northern section of the structure known today as the Spring Grove Laundry Building (see page 123).

DR. RICHARD GUNDRY AND FAMILY IN FRONT OF THE MAIN BUILDING. Dr. Gundry (at left) was medical superintendent from 1878 to 1891 and died while still in office. He made Spring Grove the first, or one of the first, of the state hospitals in the United States to abolish the use of mechanical restraints for patients. An emphasis was placed on allowing as many patients as possible to have access to the sunshine, freedom, and fresh air of the hospital's grounds.

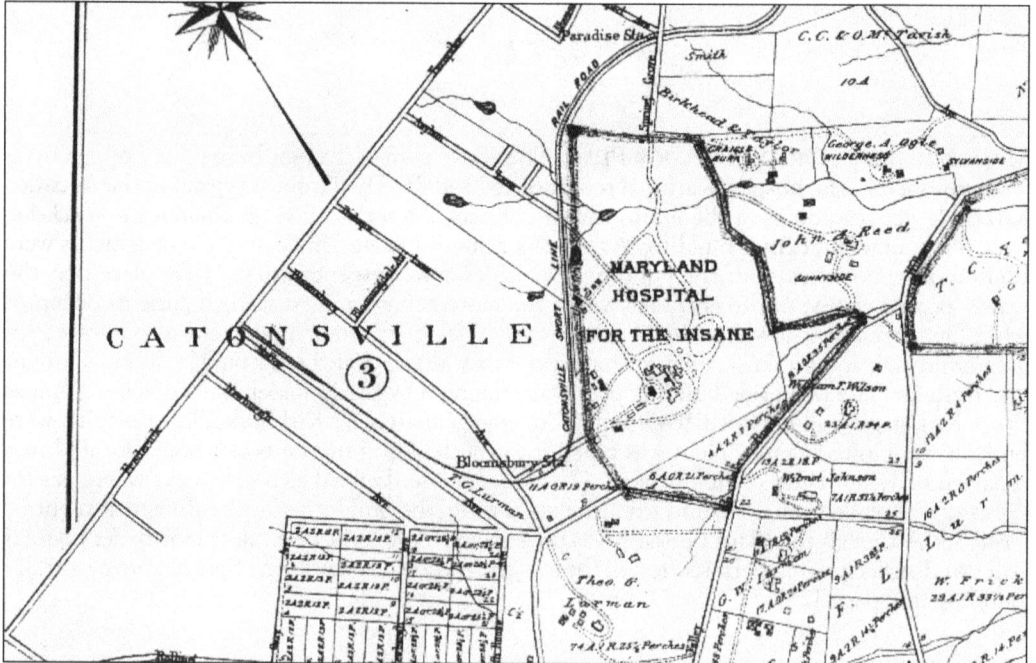

MAP, 1898. This section of a map of Catonsville shows the location of Spring Grove's original 136 acres. The Spring Grove campus today consists of approximately 190 acres that include several later acquisitions, the largest of which is a parcel of 43 acres purchased in 1909 for $12,226. The 1909 acquisition was a farm known as "Sunnyside." (The location of Sunnyside is shown above, just to the east of the hospital's property.)

24

GRAHAM FAMILY, AROUND 1890. The persons shown in this photograph are believed to be members of the family of John S. Graham, Spring Grove's clerk from 1876 to 1897.

THE BLOOMSBURY AVENUE GATEHOUSE. This still-extant gatehouse was built in the 1880s, along with two very similar dwellings, under the direction of Superintendent Richard F. Gundry. Originally known as "lodges," the three houses were reportedly at one time used as a sort of testing residence for patients who were deemed to possibly be ready for discharge.

THE PARADISE AVENUE GATEHOUSE. The poetically named Paradise Avenue Gatehouse, shown in this early view, still stands at what was once one of the main entrances to the hospital grounds. The Paradise Avenue Gatehouse has changed very little over the years and can be easily spotted from I-695, the Baltimore Beltway, on the hill just above the outer loop and between the Wilkens Avenue and Frederick Road exits.

MAIN GATEWAY AND LODGE HOUSE, 1899. This no-longer-extant gatehouse, originally called a "lodge house," once stood at the main entrance to Spring Grove. The two stone posts that held the gates at the main entrance are still standing in their original location and serve as landmarks by which to locate the approximate site of the gatehouse, now a vacant lot. A platform and a very small portion of the tracks that served the Catonsville Short Line Railroad are visible in the image's foreground.

SIX NURSES, MAIN BUILDING LAWN AROUND 1890. This glass-plate photograph can be roughly dated by the presence of a youthful Nora Coakley, the nurse who is seated at left. Coakley joined the staff in 1885. (Courtesy of Catonsville Room, Catonsville Public Library.)

NURSING STAFF ON THE NORTH LAWN OF THE MAIN BUILDING. Although the photograph is undated, it may have been taken on the occasion of Spring Grove's centennial in 1897.

NURSES AND ATTENDANTS ON THE LAWN OF THE MAIN BUILDING, 1909. In deference to the sensibilities and traditions of the time, male and female patients at Spring Grove during the 19th and early 20th centuries lived largely separate lives. The two sexes resided in entirely separate wings of the hospital and spent their days in gender-segregated job assignments. They also took their meals in separate dining rooms. In fact, male and female patients typically encountered each other only at certain hospital-sponsored social functions, such as dances or concerts, or at church services on Sundays. The identities of the subjects are as follows: from left to right, (first row) unidentified, Maud Stimmel (retired after 46 years of service), two unidentified, Nora Coakley (died in 1939 while still employed and after 54 years of service), Sadie Firming, and two unidentified; (second row) Johnny Madden, Joe Barker, Tom Skinner (supervisor), Tug Wilson, and "Shorty" Robinson; (third row) unidentified, John McNulty (retired after 45 years of service), unidentified, and ? Strolmeyer.

MALE ATTENDANTS, 1890S. These 15 men served as attendants in what was called "The Male Department." This photograph may have been taken on the occasion of the hospital's centennial in 1897.

WATERCOLOR OF SPRING GROVE. This image was reportedly painted by a patient sometime in the late 19th century. Note the game of lawn tennis depicted in the foreground. Remnants of a tennis court that was located at approximately the same spot as the one shown here can be found today behind the Spring Grove Administration Building.

WARD—FEMALE DEPARTMENT, 1899. In a plan that would definitely violate fire codes today, the wide corridors of the wards in the Main Building were used as day halls. Note the gas lighting fixtures. On close examination of the photograph, it can be seen that these fixtures had been retrofitted with electric light sockets.

MAIN BUILDING, FEMALE DEPARTMENT HALL, C. 1909. The southern wing of the Main Building was known as "The Female Department." The hospital's records indicate that at least some of the wicker furniture shown in this photograph may have been fashioned by patient labor at Spring Grove.

SIX SPRING GROVE NURSES. The ivy-covered Main Building served as the backdrop for the six nurses who posed for this photograph, probably around the dawn of the 20th century. Note the set of keys that are pinned to the waist of the nurse at the center front. Keys, a symbol of authority in 19th-century psychiatric hospitals, were sometimes prominently displayed by staff members, who generally wore them attached to their garments.

MAIN BUILDING, C. 1895. Note the fountain in the circle in front of the building. Persons who are familiar with the Spring Grove of today will recognize the circle in which the fountain was located as the traffic circle near the Administration Building's parking lot.

BASKET WEAVING AT SPRING GROVE. This undated photograph shows male patients engaged in the task of weaving wicker baskets. Repetitive tasks such as basket-weaving were considered to be therapeutic for persons who were suffering from mental illnesses. Some 7,000 willow plants were procured and planted at Spring Grove in the 1890s for the purpose of making baskets and wicker furniture.

SPRING GROVE INDUSTRIAL SHOP IN 1899. The man who can be seen standing in the background at the right was identified as George Shad, an employee. The workers shown here were engaged in making garments, shoes, and boots.

CARPENTRY SHOP, 1900. This photograph was featured in Spring Grove's annual report of 1900. Among the articles made by male patients at the hospital in that year were 140 pairs of trousers, 188 pairs of overalls, 114 coats, 494 pairs of shoes or boots, 2 tents, 586 brooms, 516 shirts, 5 razor strops, 30 pieces of furniture, 13 picture frames, 35 curtains, 77 baskets, 420 pairs of "drawers," and a holster.

MEN'S INDUSTRIAL SHOP, INTERIOR. This view shows persons engaged in various enterprises that appear to include a print shop. According to the hospital's 1903 annual report, male patients engaged in farming, carpentry, painting, upholstery, tailoring, blacksmithing, and "ward work." Gender role conformity was fairly rigidly enforced at Spring Grove at the turn of the 20th century, and female patients were generally assigned to work in the laundry, kitchen, and sewing rooms. Patients of both sexes assumed housekeeping duties and served food in the male and female refectories.

MEN'S INDUSTRIAL SHOP, INTERIOR. Shoemaking and tailoring were considered the two most important industries at the hospital in the 1890s. Almost all work was done by patient labor.

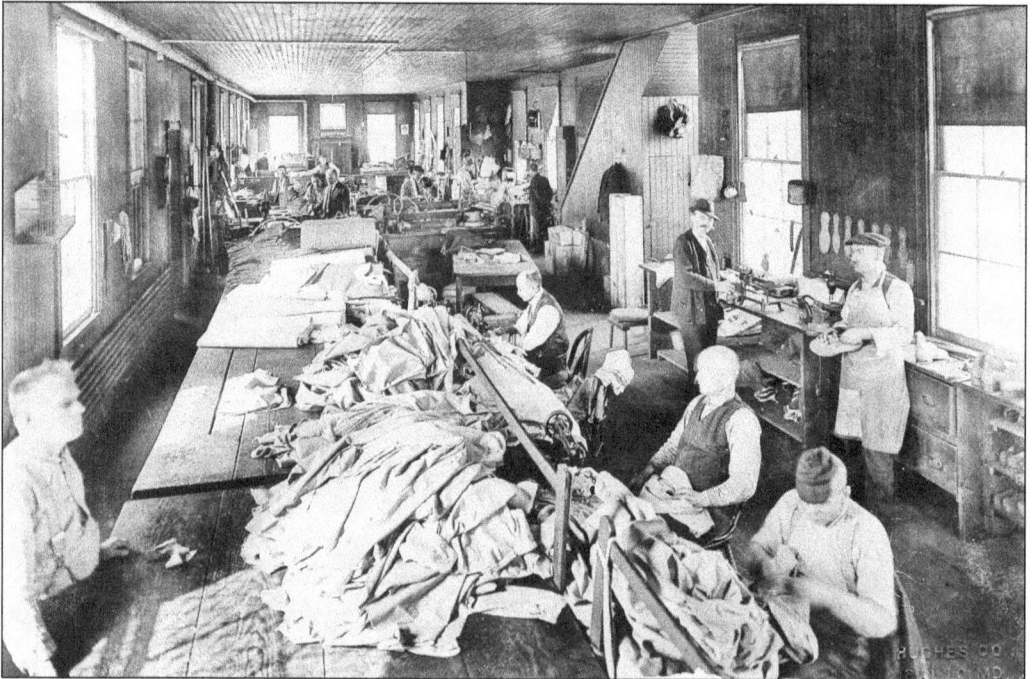

SPRING GROVE INDUSTRIAL SHOP. The hospital was dependent on patient labor and could not have functioned without it. It is interesting to note that when Spring Grove transferred its African American patients to the newly opened Hospital for the Negro Insane at Crownsville between 1911 and 1913, Spring Grove reportedly declined to transfer a certain number of the African American patients, not out of a sense of what was right, but because those particular patients held essential skills that could not be duplicated by anyone else, patients or staff, at the hospital.

FIREHOUSE AND INDUSTRIAL BUILDING, DATE UNKNOWN. The smaller building to the left is the hospital's still-extant *c.* 1872 firehouse. The larger building at right is the no-longer-extant Industrial Building (see previous page).

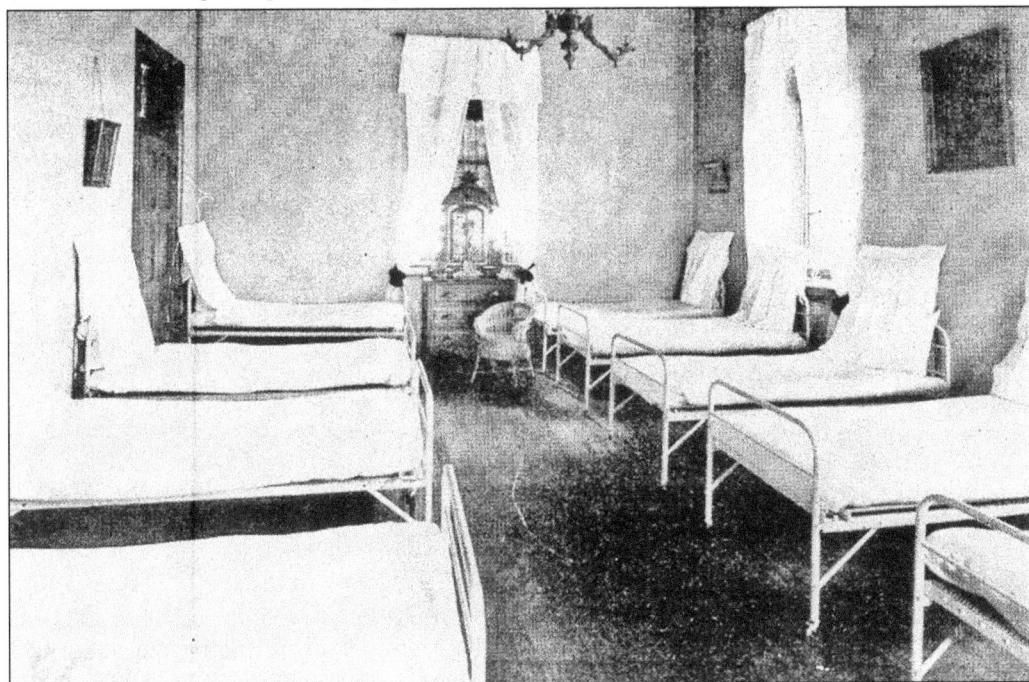

PATIENT DORMITORY, MAIN BUILDING, C. 1899. Most of the patients were accommodated in private bedrooms at the time that the Main Building opened in 1872. However, the original design did include a few dormitories for those patients who were less severely ill. Note the mirrored dresser and the gas chandelier.

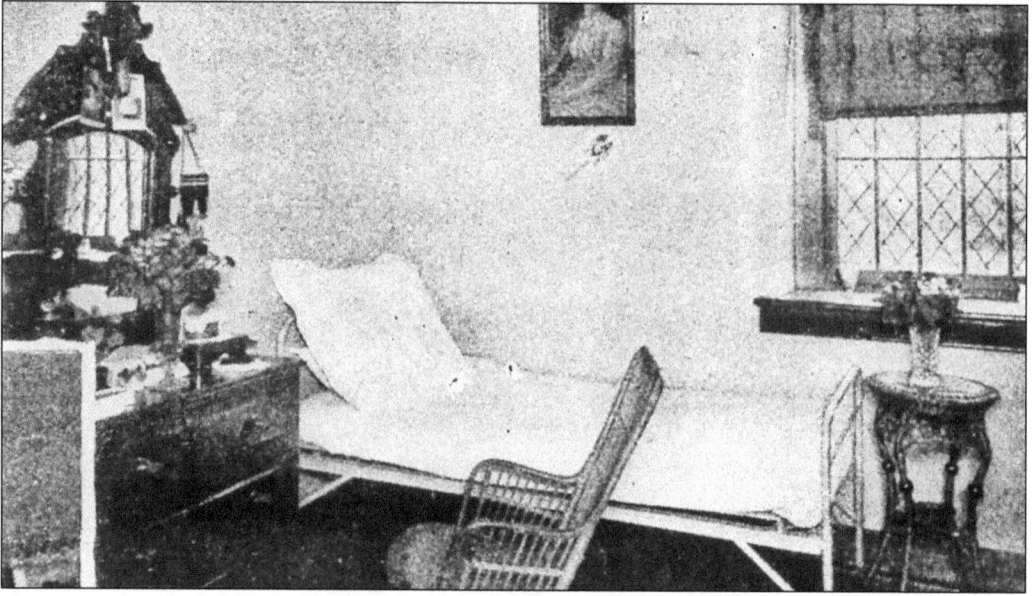

PATIENT BEDROOM, MAIN BUILDING, C. 1899. For a number of years in the 19th and very early 20th centuries, patients were typically confined to their rooms at night. Nursing staff usually went to sleep at around the same time as the patients and, in fact, sometimes slept in staff dormitories on the wards. While everyone else was asleep, the building's corridors and grounds were patrolled throughout the night by male and female "night watchmen." Originally most patients had private bedrooms.

PATIENT PARLOR, MAIN BUILDING, C. 1899. The room shown in the bottom image had originally served as one of the ward dining rooms. However, not long after the Main Building opened, two central dining rooms or "refectories" were opened in previously unoccupied space in the center of the building. Their completion allowed the dining rooms that had been located on a number of the wards to be converted to other purposes, such as dormitories or, as shown above, a patient parlor.

MAIN BUILDING AIRING COURT, AROUND 1900. These women are seen in what was called an "airing court" at the rear of the Main Building. The woman on the left can be clearly identified as a nurse by her uniform and keys.

OFFICERS OF THE HOSPITAL, C. 1899. This group of five men and a terrier are posed on the well-landscaped lawn in front of the Main Building. The man who is seen standing in the center was J. Percy Wade, M.D., superintendent. Seated at left is Robert Edward Garrett, M.D., after whom the Garrett Building at Spring Grove was named. Dr. Garrett joined the hospital as an assistant physician in 1899 and became superintendent in 1927. Standing at the right is Allan S. Graham, Spring Grove's clerk at the time.

MAYPOLE DANCE, SPRING GROVE STATE HOSPITAL. This photograph appeared in a Spring Grove postcard from the early 20th century. It is believed to have been taken during the hospital's centennial celebrations in 1897.

Spring Grove State Hospital.   Catonsvile, Md.

HELLO FROM SPRING GROVE. This image is taken from the second of the two Spring Grove postcards that are known to still exist. In a bygone era, depictions of state hospitals on postcards were not uncommon. The view is of the Main Building, and the vantage point is from the approximate location of the steps of today's Administration Building.

SPRING GROVE NURSING STAFF AT THE ENTRANCE TO THE MAIN BUILDING, AROUND 1915. The circular object that resembles a clock and that can be viewed in the right background seems to have been a device that continuously recorded and timed the opening and closing of the building's front door, for security and monitoring purposes.

SPRING GROVE MALE ATTENDANTS AT THE ENTRANCE TO THE MAIN BUILDING. This photograph and the one immediately above it were obviously taken in succession. The man in the dark uniform was longtime employee John McNulty. He is dressed in what was described as the "Sunday Dress Uniform of Attending Staff."

MAIN BUILDING FACADE. This photograph was probably taken in the 1910s. The front portion of the center section of the building, shown here, was primarily used as offices and staff living quarters.

NURSES ON THE GROUNDS OF SPRING GROVE. This glass-plate photograph is believed to date from the late 1870s or early 1880s.

SPRING GROVE LAUNDRY, C. 1909. The machines seen here were driven by belts that led to a series of overhead cams and shafts that, in turn, were powered by the engine that can be faintly distinguished in the cage at the right rear. The large tubs seen along the right wall were designed to tumble—once they were filled with laundry, water, and soap. Note the large laundry press and folding table at the left rear. This still-extant structure was built in 1907.

SELECTED VIEWS OF THE SPRING GROVE GROUNDS, 1890S. These three photographs of the hospital grounds were displayed against an art nouveau backdrop in the hospital's annual report of 1899. This same report includes a passage that reads: "Golf Links have been constructed on the lawn, stretching out towards the woods, and have been the means of affording pleasant diversion for many of the athletic patients of both sexes." The hospital's grounds have always had a therapeutic benefit. In 1875, Dr. J. R. Conrad, who was at that time Spring Grove's resident physician, wrote: "It is very important for Insane patients to exercise in the open air as much as possible, not only for the benefit of their daily general health, but also for the reason that it breaks the monotony of the confinement of Hospital life, promotes sleep, calms nervous excitement, and give opportunity for a complete ventilation of the Halls and rooms by natural ventilation."

AFRICAN AMERICAN PATIENTS AT SPRING GROVE. At the dawn of the 20th century, African American male patients at Spring Grove often lived in tents on the hospital's grounds. Although it might be assumed that the tents were used only during the summer months, an annual report from the period notes that the men sometimes lived in the tents for as many as eight months out of the year. The practice was partially attributable to overcrowding in the Main Building. In addition, around 1900, such tents were used in a number of hospitals (including Spring Grove) to isolate patients who had infectious diseases, such as tuberculosis. The hospital's records indicate that the tents were manufactured at Spring Grove by patients.

COTTAGE FOR "COLORED WOMEN," 1906. The top image shows a group of nine African American female patients and a nurse at the entrance of what was called the "Cottage for Colored Women." The two-story structure was completed in March 1906 at a cost of $6,799. According to the annual report of 1906, the building housed 25 African American female patients. The upper floor was used as sleeping quarters, and the lower floor included a sitting room ("for those who do not work") and a dining room. The Hospital for the Negro Insane of Maryland, later known as Crownsville State Hospital, was founded in 1910, and by 1913, almost all of Spring Grove's African American patients had been transferred there. After 1913, the above building became known as the "TB Cottage" and was used to isolate white female patients who had tuberculosis (bottom image). This no-longer-extant structure was located immediately behind the Main Building, in the exact spot where the lawn shop stands today.

HOSPITAL FOR THE NEGRO INSANE OF MARYLAND, LATER CROWNSVILLE STATE HOSPITAL. The original caption for this image reads: "Patients engaged in building a new road from the hospital site to the temporary building." Crownsville State Hospital's first patients were 16 African American men transferred from Spring Grove in 1911. In the following year, most of the remaining male patients of African descent were transferred from Spring Grove to Crownsville. Initially the men lived in temporary structures on the grounds of Crownsville, and records indicate that they contributed much of the labor that went into building the hospital. African American female patients were transferred from Spring Grove to Crownsville one year later, in 1913. Shamefully, Maryland didn't complete the reintegration of its state hospitals until 1963. Spring Grove was reintegrated two years earlier, in 1961.

PATIENTS ASSISTING IN THE CONSTRUCTION OF CROWNSVILLE STATE HOSPITAL. This photograph is labeled, "Patients laboring [in the] construction of [the] Industrial Shop." It is likely that at least some of the persons shown in this photograph were patients who had been transferred to Crownsville from Spring Grove in 1911 and 1912.

PROCESSING TOBACCO. The men shown in this picture were processing tobacco at Crownsville State Hospital. The photograph is undated, but it is believed to date from the mid-1910s.

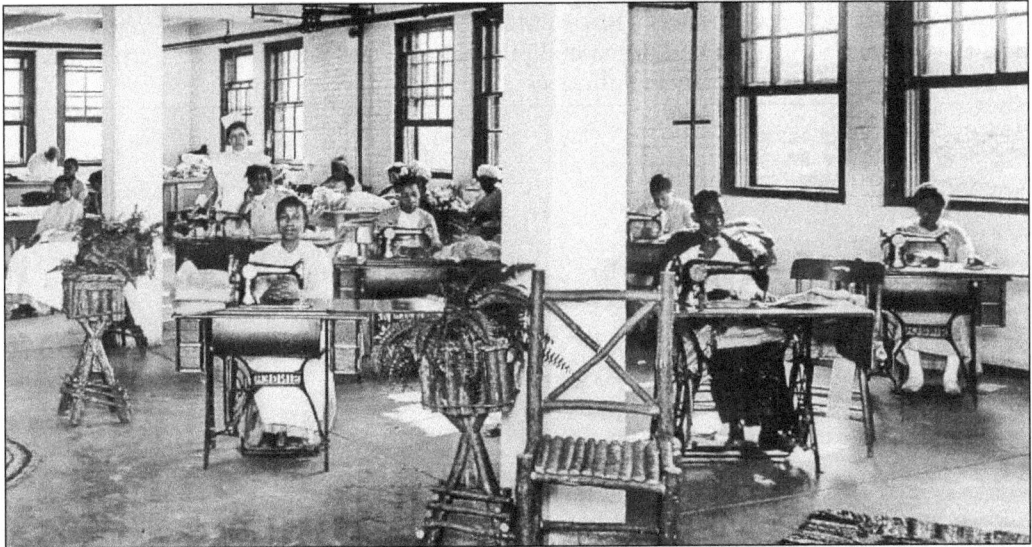

MARYLAND'S STATE HOSPITALS UNDER JIM CROW. This undated photograph of the women's sewing room at Crownsville State Hospital is from sometime after 1913, the year that Maryland's state hospitals were segregated. Spring Grove patient population throughout the 19th century seems to have always included African American patients. For example, the hospital's 1849 annual report notes that as of the end of December of that year, 10 of the hospital's 152 patients were African Americans. Nine of those 10 patients were described as having been free, while one of the patients was reported to have been a slave. Subsequent hospital reports indicate that the individual wards within Spring Grove were racially integrated at least into the late 1880s. However, segregated units for African American patients had been established in the Main Building by the mid-1890s.

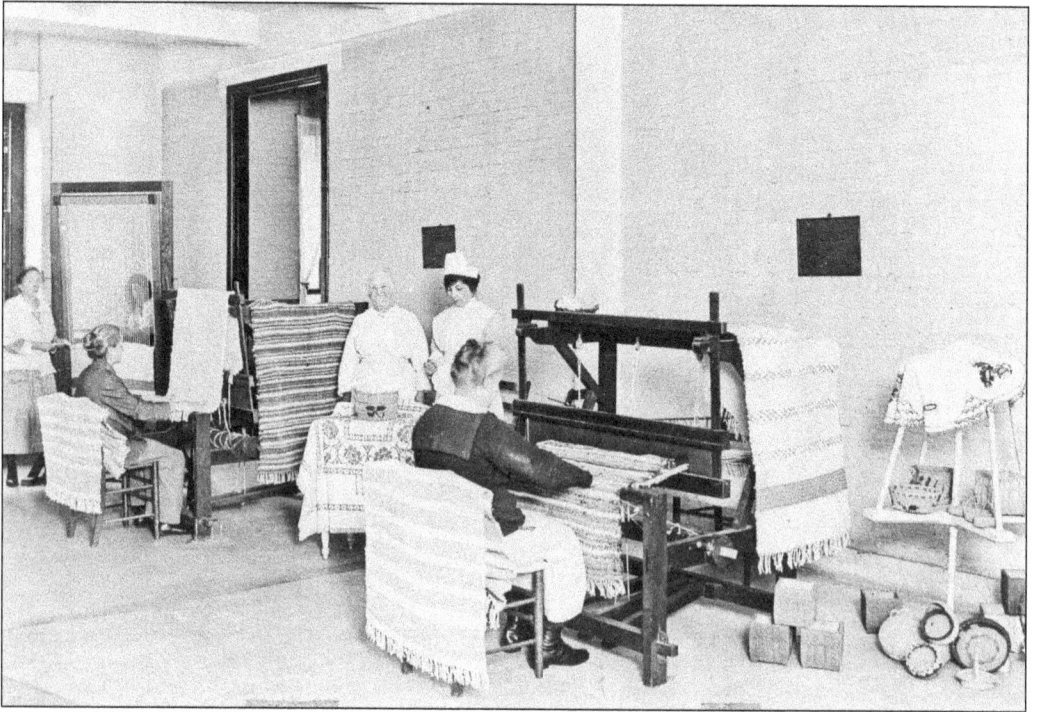

WOMEN'S OCCUPATIONAL THERAPY ROOM, MAIN BUILDING. The principles of moral therapy held that human occupation and purposeful physical activities were curative, particularly for those who were suffering from mental illnesses.

FLORIST'S DWELLING, C. 1915. "In 1882–1883," according to the 1893 Board of Managers Report, "a stone cottage was built for the use of the gardener. The stone used in this and other buildings was quarried on the hospital grounds; all necessary excavations and grading were done by hospital attendants and patients."

LILY PONDS, SPRING GROVE STATE HOSPITAL. According to a label that was found with this undated photograph, these ponds were located in what was then the southeastern portion of the Spring Grove campus. An early aerial view of the campus suggests that they may have been situated near the site of today's Tawes Building. (Courtesy of Catonsville Room, Catonsville Public Library.)

HORSE-DRAWN WAGON AT SPRING GROVE. The Valley Road entrance was used as the primary route to and from the hospital's farm "colony" and to Wilkens Avenue.

FIRE BRIGADE, C. 1900. Based upon the apparent lack of urgency with which the subjects of this photograph seem to be approaching their task, it may be assumed that they were only engaged in a drill. The scene is the rear of the Main Building. Records from the period report that the Spring Grove fire brigade assisted the Baltimore County Fire Department in extinguishing fires in nearby parts of Catonsville. On close examination, several nurses can be faintly seen at the windows.

FIREHOUSE, C. 1897. Spring Grove's 19th-century firehouse still stands, largely unchanged, in its original location. At one time, it held the hospital's firefighting equipment—one piece of which, a horse-drawn hose wagon, can be seen in this image through the building's open doors.

MAIN BUILDING SUN PARLOR, C. 1915. The Main Building's sun parlors were glass-enclosed and heated so they could be used year-round. According to a former Main Building staff member, there was an ongoing problem associated with the fact that amorous male patients would periodically climb the sides of the sun parlors to visit the female patients.

PATIENTS BUILDING A ROAD. This undated photograph shows a group of patients and supervising employees engaged in the construction of a new road at Spring Grove. It is believed that this photograph was taken about 1908.

OCCUPATIONAL THERAPY IN THE MAIN BUILDING. The needlework on the two pillows in the foreground reads, "It's a Long, Long Way to Tipperary" and "Everyone is in Slumberland but You and Me"—both popular songs from the 1910s. The small banner seen hanging at the top features a 48-star U.S. flag, which would indicate that this undated photograph was taken sometime after Arizona entered the Union in 1914.

WOMEN'S SEWING ROOM, MAIN BUILDING. These women displayed the fruits of their labors in this undated image. The nurse, seen wearing a white cap, has been identified as Sadie Furman.

OFFICERS, SPRING GROVE STATE HOSPITAL, 1909. From left to right are (seated) J. Percy Wade, M.D., superintendent; and S. Thomas Brown, the hospital's steward; (standing) Arthur L. Wright, M.D., the hospital's pathologist; Compton Graham, who held the title of clerk; and Robert P. Winterode, M.D., and R. Edward Garrett, M.D., both of whom were assistant physicians at the time.

EXHIBITION OF SPRING GROVE ART AND HANDICRAFTS. This display of various works of arts, needlework, furniture, and other items created by Spring Grove patients may have been part of the festivities that marked the hospital's centennial in 1897. The setting is not known but is probably the basement of the Main Building, which had been the location of the women's industrial shop.

PATIENT HISTORY FROM 1897. The individual referenced in this report was a 45-year-old man who was suffering from visual hallucinations and suicidal thoughts when he was admitted to Spring Grove in January 1897. It was noted that the patient wasn't sleeping, talked incessantly and irrationally, and had tried to set his house on fire. The notation "Col" next to the patient's name on the report indicates that he was African American.

Three

RAPID EXPANSION AND GROWTH 1920–1941

Throughout the 1920s and 1930s, the number of admissions to Spring Grove substantially surpassed the number of discharges each year, and the hospital responded through a series of new construction projects. Major structures completed between 1920 and 1941 included the Foster-Wade Building, the Hillcrest Building, the Bland-Bryant Building, the Garrett Infirmary Building, the five Stone Cottages and their central dining room and kitchen, and the Rice Auditorium.

In 1933, at the depth of the Great Depression, the hospital's census reached 1,565 patients and the number of annual admissions hit 535. Of the 274 patients discharged in 1933, a total of 104 were declared to have recovered fully, while 138 patients were discharged as "improved" but not fully recovered. An additional 71 patients were discharged as "unimproved." One hundred thirty-four patients died in 1933, many of infectious diseases such as tuberculosis and pneumonia.

To meet the dietary needs of the increased numbers of patients, it became necessary to expand the hospital's farming operations, and during the first three decades of the 20th century, the hospital's land holdings more than quadrupled—from 136 acres to 616 acres. Much of the farmland that was acquired by Spring Grove during this period is now the University of Maryland, Baltimore County (UMBC).

In the days before Social Security and other public entitlement programs, some of the individuals at Spring Grove were in the hospital simply because they were dispossessed. While conditions at the ever-more-crowded Spring Grove and other state psychiatric hospitals were not always the best, circumstances were typically much worse at the county-run almshouses and asylums. Accordingly indigent individuals often selected the state hospital as a place to live, even if they didn't truly have a mental illness.

Spring Grove opened a nursing school in 1929, in the 1930s, began joint research programs with the Johns Hopkins and University of Maryland Hospitals. Psychoanalytic techniques were used in some cases, while interventions such as sedative medications, hypnotherapy, and hydrotherapy were used in others. Occupational therapy remained the most important treatment, and most patients continued to work on the farm or in one of the industrial shops. In 1935, the annual cost per patient was just $198.

SUPERINTENDENT'S OFFICE, MAIN BUILDING. This photograph, from the early 20th century, shows the superintendent, Dr. J. Percy Wade, at his desk. Note the two candlestick telephones that can be faintly distinguished on Dr. Wade's desk. The hospital installed telephone service in 1896.

THE FOSTER CLINIC, FRONT VIEW, C. 1920. Until the A. D. Foster Clinic opened on July 1, 1920, almost all of Spring Grove's patients were cared for in the Main Building. Persons familiar with the Foster-Wade Building today will note upon close examination of this photograph that the left half of the building appears to be missing. That is because the Foster-Wade Building was constructed in two phases, and the first section to be completed was occupied before the second phase was begun. The center building and the eastern wing (seen here) were built in between 1914 and 1920. The western wing was constructed between 1926 and 1928.

FOSTER CLINIC UNDER CONSTRUCTION. Although it was known as the Psychopathic Building when the cornerstone was laid in 1914, the building was renamed the A. D. Foster Clinic in 1919, while still under construction, in memory of Arthur D. Foster. Foster had been the secretary and treasurer of the hospital's board of managers for many years. The building was renamed for a second time in 1928, when the western wing, sometimes referred to as the Wade Wing, was completed. The second renaming was to honor J. Percy Wade, M.D., the former superintendent who had been responsible for the building's construction and who had retired in the previous year. Dr. Wade was present at the Foster-Wade Building's dedication in 1928. The box-like structure in the foreground was the top of an airshaft for a pedestrian tunnel that led to the Main Building.

55

THE FOSTER CLINIC FROM THE REAR, C. 1920. This photograph was taken before the Wade Wing was added to the building. Note that the land behind the building is under cultivation. While the majority of the hospital's farmland during much of the 20th century was eventually situated on the portion of the grounds that are now part of the University of Maryland, Baltimore County (UMBC) campus, large portions of the main campus were also used to grow crops.

FOSTER CLINIC SUN PORCH, C. 1920. The sun porches of the Foster Clinic (later known as the Foster-Wade Building) were used as day halls. Between 1920 and 1925, prior to the opening of the Perry Point Veteran's Hospital, the Foster Clinic was used to treat servicemen and World War I veterans.

MEN'S OCCUPATIONAL THERAPY. This photograph shows men working in an industrial occupation shop in the lower level of the Foster Clinic (now known as the Foster-Wade Building) in the early 1920s. Weaving was considered to be a particularly therapeutic activity.

BLAND-BRYANT BUILDING. The Bland-Bryant Building was built in 1930 at a cost of $460,000. It originally held 430 male convalescent patients. This rendering of the building was drawn by its architect, Henry Powell Hopkins.

THE HILLCREST BUILDING OPENS, 1922. In 1921, Superintendent J. Percy Wade's vision of a treatment facility for the criminally insane was rewarded when the state appropriated $135,500 for the construction of a "Criminal Building" at Spring Grove. The Hillcrest Building's debut was a historic event in that it marked the opening of the first state psychiatric hospital building in America to be designed specifically for the containment and rehabilitation of criminally insane patients. Formally named the Spring Grove Psychopathic Hospital for Criminals, but more commonly known as the Hillcrest Building or Criminal Building, it opened in March 1922. At its opening, 25 patients were transferred from other parts of Spring Grove, and the balance of the building's remaining 60 beds were filled by 35 inmates who were transferred from the Maryland Penitentiary and House of Corrections. (Courtesy of Papers of Henry Powell Hopkins; Special Collections, University of Maryland Libraries.)

HILLCREST BUILDING, 1931. Architect Henry Powell Hopkins designed specific security features that were masked by ornate architectural details. The windows, doors, and stairs were made and designed with special materials that would prove difficult to tamper with or damage. Several of the eye-catching visual components to Hillcrest's exterior included copper flashing along the roof's crickets and cupola, a marble entranceway, brass knobs on the ends of entryway railings, tooth-like dentils along the cornice, and a wood-carving that was affixed to the center gable. At the time, such architectural features were considered to be both unique and progressive in a building designed to house mentally ill persons who had been charged with violent crimes. The Hillcrest Building design was published in the journal *Architectural Forum* in December 1922. Between 1921 and 1961, Hopkins designed many of Spring Grove's buildings, including the Hillcrest, Bland-Bryant, Garrett, White, Hamilton, and Dayhoff Buildings, along with the Stone Cottages, Red Brick Cottages, the Employees' Cafeteria Building, and the Superintendent's House.

HILLCREST BUILDING PHYSICIAN OFFICE, 1931. The man seated at the desk was a Mr. Price, the Hillcrest Building supervisor at the time. Standing at center, in the white coat and dark tie, was William Franklin Wheatley, a respected member of the Hillcrest Building staff. Wheatley's wife, Ella, was a Spring Grove nursing attendant who worked in the Main Building.

HILLCREST BUILDING SUPERVISOR AND PHYSICIAN, 1931. These two men have been identified as Dr. Brown (seated) and Mr. Price, the building's supervisor. The setting is the physician's office on the building's first floor.

GREENHOUSE IN 1921. Several greenhouses were built at Spring Grove over the years, including one that was built in 1904 near the gardener's cottage, at the site that is now occupied by the Maryland Psychiatric Research Center headquarters building. This photograph was labeled "Foster Clinic Industrial Occupation."

HORTICULTURE AS OCCUPATIONAL THERAPY. The man seen standing in the foreground was a Mr. LeClair, an occupational therapy instructor who worked with veterans at Spring Grove in the period following World War I.

PIGGERY C. 1920. Over the years, Spring Grove operated piggeries in several locations. The one seen above was located on the main campus, in the area that is today occupied by the Superintendent's House. The hospital also operated a piggery near the location where now stands the Walker Avenue police station.

HARVEST TIME AT SPRING GROVE. This undated photograph was taken on the Spring Grove farm, probably sometime in the 1920s. Younger male patients were typically assigned to work in the fields, milk the cows, slop pigs, and attend to other farm-related chores.

SPRING GROVE FARM COLONY, C. 1927. Originally, all of Spring Grove's farmlands were located in the lands surrounding the Main Building. The first major expansion of Spring Grove's property beyond the original 136 acres occurred in 1909, when the hospital purchased a 43-acre farm known as Sunnyside. (Today the Dayhoff and White Buildings are situated on land that was part of the Sunnyside purchase.) The new land was used to expand Spring Grove's farming operations, but as the hospital's census continued to increase, the additional 43 acres soon proved to be inadequate. In response, the hospital substantially expanded its landholding during the 1910s and 1920s by acquiring most of the land that today is the campus of the University of Maryland, Baltimore County (UMBC). By 1930, the hospital owned 616 acres, of which 306 were under cultivation. Large-scale farming operations stopped in the late 1950s, and the farm colony property was transferred to the University of Maryland in 1965.

ROBERT EDWARD GARRETT, M.D. Garrett was superintendent of Spring Grove State Hospital from 1928 to 1936. The Garrett Infirmary Building was named in his honor.

THE HILLTOP HOUSE. This no-longer-extant structure was part of a 36-acre parcel known as the Cockey Estate. It was purchased by Spring Grove in 1917 as part of the hospital's drive to expand the number of acres that it had under cultivation. This and a number of other houses in Spring Grove's "Farm Colony" were used to house employees and, in some instances, convalescent patients. Hilltop House burned to the ground on New Year's Day 1959.

WALKER HOUSE. Built around the time of the Civil War, the Walker House was a property that was owned by Spring Grove and used for employee housing for a number of years. Ultimately the home was acquired by the University of Maryland, Baltimore County, where it served as the president's home for a short time. It has since been demolished.

AERIAL VIEWS, SPRING GROVE STATE HOSPITAL, 1927. The top image shows the back of the Main Building. The Foster-Wade Building is seen in the left background. The various buildings in the foreground include the horse stables, the Industrial Building, the TB Building, and the carpentry and bake shops. In the bottom image, the larger building on the left is the Main Building. The building on the right side of the image is the Foster-Wade Building.

FOSTER-WADE AND MAIN BUILDINGS, AERIAL VIEW. In 1927, the year this photograph was taken, there were only two major patient-care buildings on Spring Grove's main campus: the Main Building (started in 1853 and completed in 1872) and the Foster-Wade Building (started in 1914 and completed in 1928). The only other major building of the period, the c. 1922 Hillcrest or "Criminal" Building was located about a mile to the south, in the middle of the hospital's farm colony.

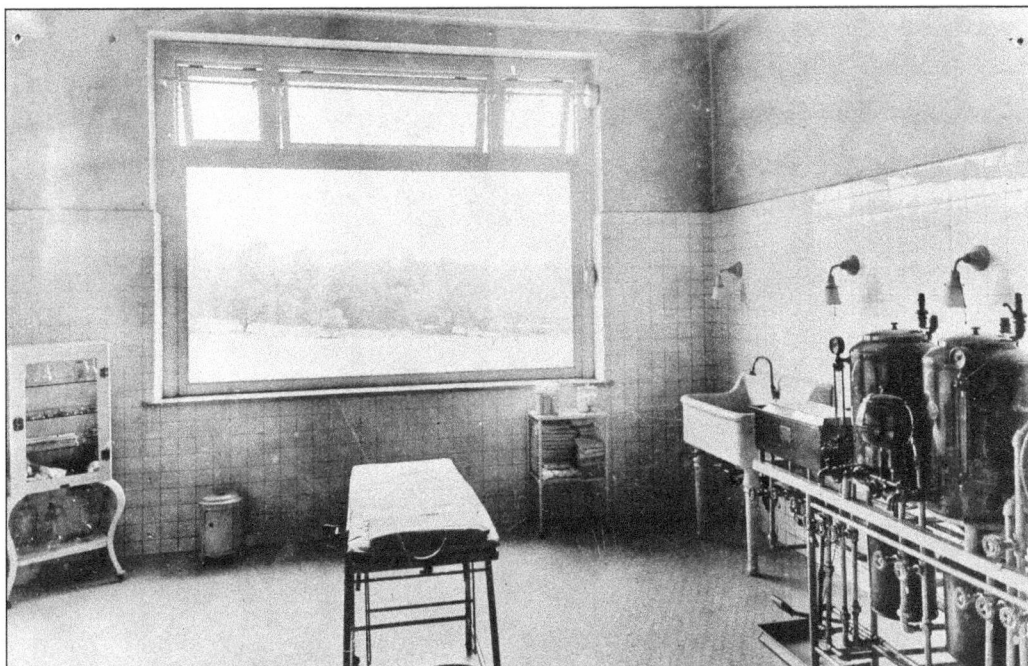

FOSTER CLINIC OPERATING ROOM. This photograph was taken sometime before 1928, the year the building known as the Foster Clinic was renamed the Foster-Wade Building. Note the large plate-glass window at the far end of the room. Sources of abundant natural illumination were designed into the operating rooms of the period because gaslight usually wasn't sufficiently bright and electric lighting sources were often unreliable.

THE FOSTER-WADE BUILDING UNDER CONSTRUCTION. The Foster-Wade Building's cornerstone reads, "Psychopathic Building 1914." The term "psychopathic" referred to forms of mental illnesses that were considered to be more amenable to active treatment.

FOSTER-WADE BUILDING CORRIDOR, DATE UNKNOWN. This photograph, probably taken around the time of World War I, shows a corridor of the eastern (or Foster) wing of what was then called the Foster Clinic. Patient bedrooms, bathrooms, treatment rooms, and staff offices lined the hallways on each side. Each of the building's six wards also had a day room and a sun porch.

LOBBY, FOSTER-WADE BUILDING, C. 1920. Note the two glass display cases along the wall in the right background. The two windows, seen in the background, and the wall that contained them were removed when the Wade Wing was added to the building between 1926 and 1928.

MEN'S WARD, FOSTER-WADE BUILDING. This photograph shows one of the sun porches in the 1926–1928 addition to the Foster-Wade Building. The hospital's current 10-year plan calls for the renovation and reuse of this historic building.

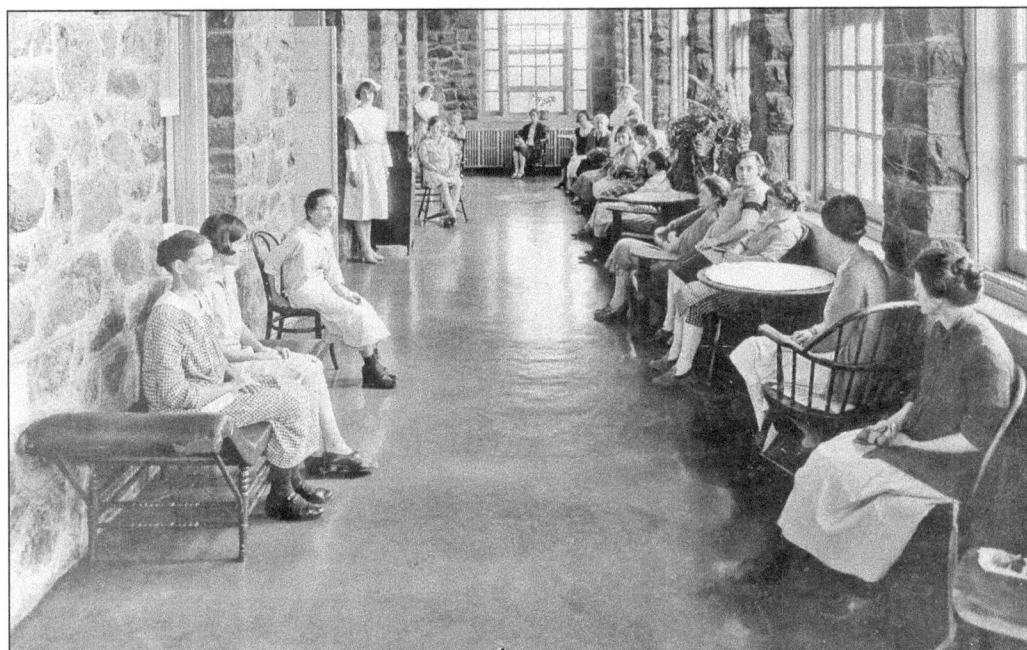

FOSTER-WADE BUILDING, C. 1928. This photograph was taken in a sun porch on one of the upper floors of the Foster-Wade Building. Between 1920, when the partially completed building was opened, and 1928, when it was completed, the building housed male patients only. However, upon the completion of the building, the men's wards were relocated to the newly built western wing, and female patients began to be admitted to the wards in the older (eastern) wing, shown here.

BLAND-BRYANT BUILDING, EARLY 1930S. This photograph of the Bland-Bryant Building was taken at about the time that the building was completed. Originally it held six large wards for convalescent male patients. Today it is the site of the headquarters of the Maryland Office of Health Care Quality.

MAIN BUILDING FACADE, 1920S. The vintage touring sedan that is visible at the left is parked directly under the windows of the superintendent's office.

GRADUATING CLASS OF 1930. This photograph was taken on the steps of the Foster-Wade Building, a popular location for pictures of the graduating classes of the Spring Grove State Hospital Training School for Nurses.

MAIN BUILDING PATIENT PARLOR IN 1931. The woman seen standing at the left of the photograph was Ella Belle Wheatly. Wheatly was a well-loved nurse in the Main Building for a number of years. Her husband, William Wheatly, was an attendant who worked in the Hillcrest Building.

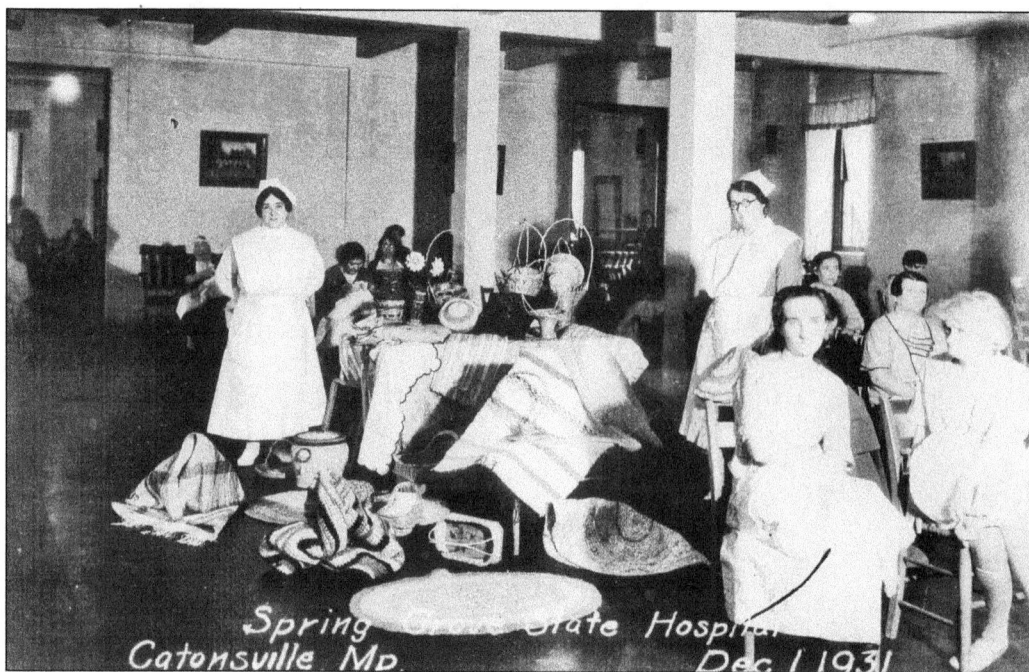

WOMEN'S OCCUPATIONAL THERAPY SHOP, 1931. The woman standing at left was Nora Coakley, Main Building nursing supervisor. The woman standing on the right was Ella Belle Wheatley.

NURSING STAFF, 1931. These 16 nurses posed for the camera on one of the sun parlors of the Main Building. Nora Coakley, the Main Building nursing supervisor, is seen seated in the center of the first row. Ella Wheatley is the nurse seated immediately to the right of her. Wheatley and her husband gave their daughter Wheatley's first name, Ella, and combined it with Coakley's first name, Nora. The daughter, Ella Nora (Wheatley) Hoerl, has worked for Spring Grove in various capacities since the 1960s.

FOSTER-WADE BUILDING SUN PORCHES, 1931. Shown here are sun porches on one of the women's wards (east wing) and one of the men's wards (west wing) in December 1931. Abundant sources of light and plenty of fresh air were considered to be essential to the promotion of both good mental and physical health. Early buildings at Spring Grove were designed to include these elements.

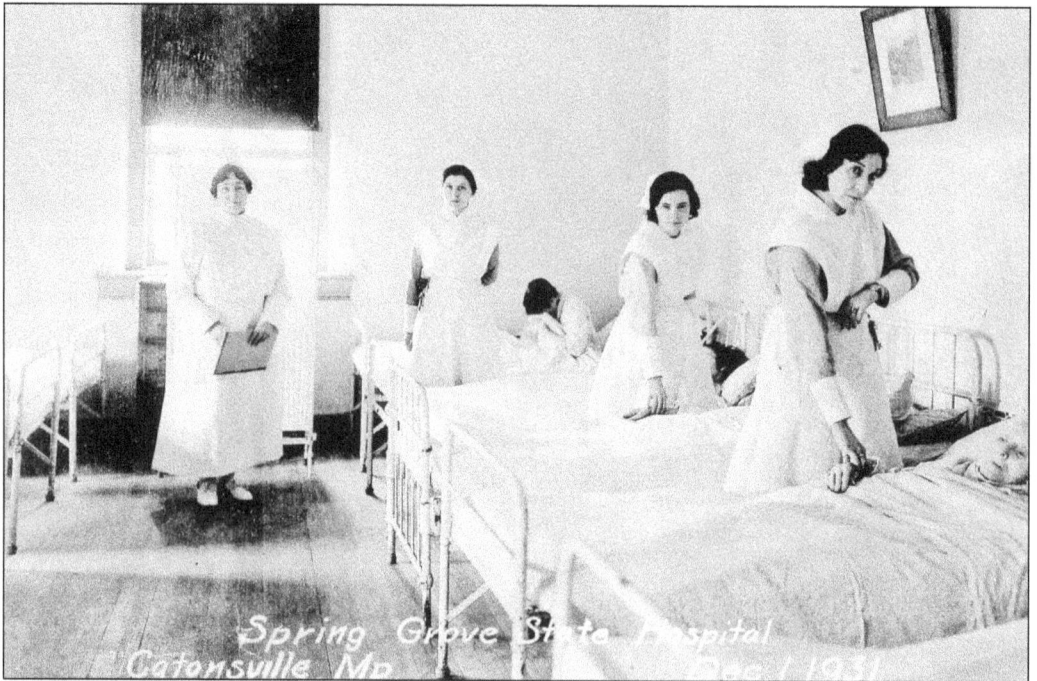

MAIN BUILDING DORMITORY. This obviously posed photograph was taken on an infirmary ward in 1931.

THE GARRETT INFIRMARY BUILDING UNDER CONSTRUCTION, C. 1932. The Garrett Building was named after Dr. Robert Edward Garrett, the man who was Spring Grove's superintendent at the time the building was built. It cost $200,000 and was designed to hold 168 beds. In addition to its infirmary wards, it held an operating room, a radiology suite, a laboratory, a sterile supply suite, isolation rooms, and the hospital's morgue. Like all major Spring Grove buildings erected before the 1950s, the Garrett Building also held living quarters for staff members.

POWER PLANT, 1932. By the early 1930s, the original 1853 boiler house was no longer adequate to meet the demands of Spring Grove's new buildings and ever-expanding needs. Accordingly, a new power plant was constructed at the western end of the main campus in 1932. As it does today, the power plant generated steam that was then piped to each of the buildings through a network of underground conduits. Coal was delivered via a spur connected to the Catonsville Short Line Railroad, a local line that ran between downtown Baltimore and Catonsville. The power plant also held ice-making machines, which made blocks of ice that were placed in front of electric fans and used to cool the wards in the summertime.

SPRING GROVE DAIRY BARN, C. 1930. This barn was located on a site that today is occupied by the University of Maryland, Baltimore County (UMBC). Much of the land upon which UMBC stands was once used as a pasture for Spring Grove's milk cows, horses, and other farm animals.

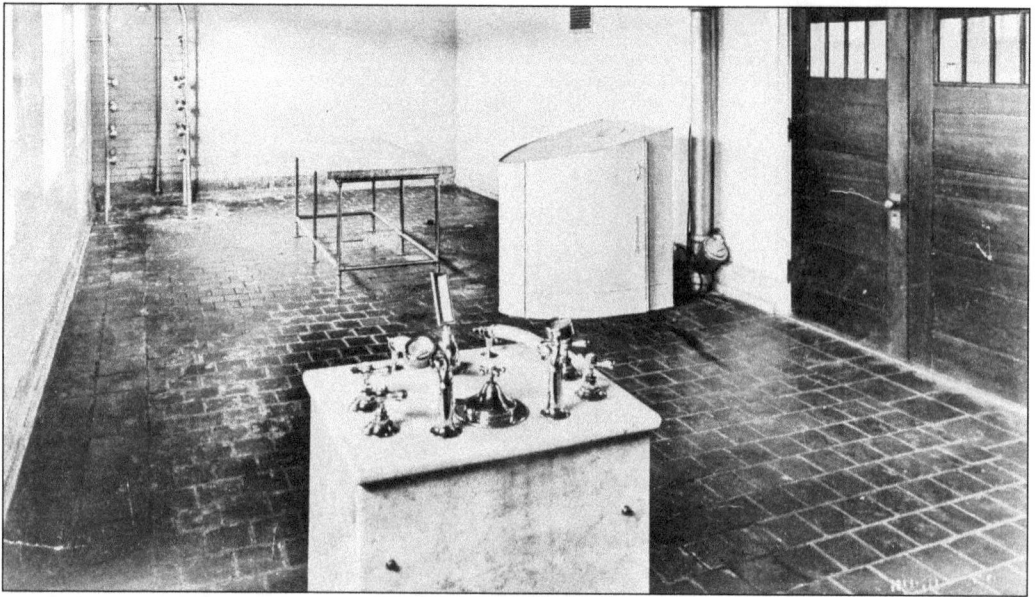

HYDROTHERAPY ROOM AT SPRING GROVE. Running water has always been known to be particularly effective in soothing distressed or tense persons, and the therapeutic use of water, known as hydrotherapy, was a widely applied form of treatment in psychiatric hospitals in the 19th and 20th centuries. The fixture in the upper left corner was called a "needle shower" because water was expelled with a fair amount of force through multiple showerheads that surrounded the occupant. The cylindrical object at the right was called a "vapor" or "cabinet bath." The above photograph shows the hydrotherapy suite located on the lower level of the Foster-Wade Building. A massage therapy room was located next door to it.

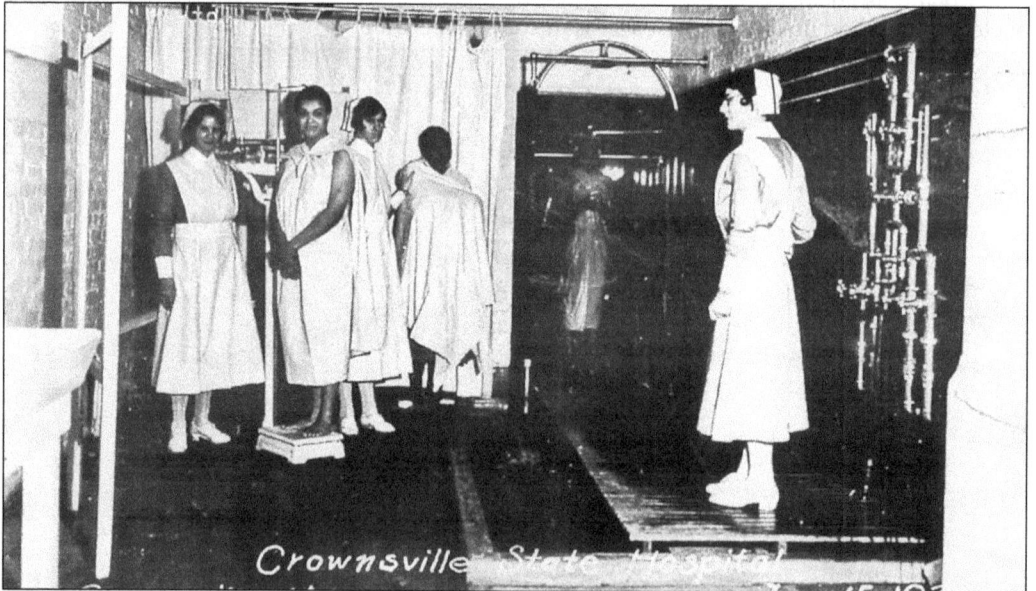

HYDROTHERAPY ROOM AT NEARBY CROWNSVILLE HOSPITAL CENTER, 1932. This photograph shows a hydrotherapy room at Crownsville State Hospital, Spring Grove's sister facility. In 2004, Crownsville Hospital Center was consolidated into Spring Grove and Springfield Hospital Centers, thus strengthening the historic ties between the three historic facilities.

THE STONE COTTAGES. These beautiful Stone Cottages were built as quarters for convalescent women patients. The two buildings in the bottom image, Cottages C and D, were built in 1935. The larger building seen at center of the group in the foreground of the above aerial view was added in 1938 to serve as the central dining room and kitchen for the complex. Two additional Stone Cottage buildings, Cottage E and F, were built in 1940. Cottage G, which is seen in the lower left corner of the upper image, was built in 1941. The five Stone Cottages were designed to hold 502 patients and, together with the central dining room and kitchen, cost $692,000.

THE COTTAGE FOR CHRONICALLY DISTURBED FEMALES. This building, known today as Stone Cottage G, was originally built to house those female patients who were found to be particularly behaviorally disturbed. Cottage G was built in 1941, but because of a steel shortage related to the military buildup for World War II, the installation of the pitched roof that had been designed for it was postponed until after the war. In use today as the site headquarters of the hospital's Information Technology Department, the building is still missing its pitched roof and, therefore, doesn't visually match the other four Stone Cottages.

MAIN BUILDING WARD, 1921. The above photograph appeared in the hospital's annual report in 1921, evidently to show off the building's recently installed tin ceilings. The furniture is believed to have been manufactured at Spring Grove by Spring Grove patients.

ARTIST'S RENDERING OF THE RICE AUDITORIUM, C. 1934. The building that is commonly known today as the Rice Auditorium was originally named the Thomas-Rice Auditorium in honor of two members of the Spring Grove State Hospital Board of Managers: Robert W. Thomas and G. Herbert Rice. The following passage appeared in a Spring Grove nursing school publication: "The new auditorium building is now finished; it contains two floors. The upper one will be used as an amusement and lecture hall, with a seating of 750. The floor space [is] sixty by one hundred and four feet and [is] four times as large as the one now in use. The lower floor will be used for an occupational therapy department, and will afford much more space than the old one." (*The Beacon*, 1936.)

RICE AUDITORIUM AT SPRING GROVE. This more recent photograph shows the interior of the largely unchanged Rice Auditorium. Today the Rice Auditorium is the location of a historic theater organ regularly used to give concerts for patients, staff, and visitors.

CHANDELIER, RICE AUDITORIUM LOBBY. The *c.* 1934 Rice Auditorium has a number of interesting art deco details. It remains largely unchanged today and is still in active use for patient and staff activities, which include concerts, parties, celebrations, meetings, and educational activities.

THE ORIGINAL AUDITORIUM, MAIN BUILDING. This undated photograph from the hospital's annual report of 1909 shows the original amusement hall, located on the second floor of the center section of the Main Building. The Main Building Amusement Hall was converted to a patient dining room after the Rice Auditorium was opened.

STAFF LOUNGE, MAIN BUILDING, C. 1920. Living quarters for employees were included on the upper floors of a number of the early buildings, including the Main Building, the Foster-Wade Building, the Garrett Building, and the Bland-Bryant Building. Typically staff members were given private or semi-private bedrooms. However, higher ranking staff members, such as physicians, sometimes lived in suites that included a sitting room, one or two bedrooms, and a private bath.

DAY ROOM, STONE COTTAGE F. This photograph was probably taken sometime during the 1950s, but is one of the few images of the interiors of the c. 1930s Stone Cottages when they were in use by patients. The wooden chairs were made at Spring Grove; one that is similar to the ones shown here is on display in the hospital's museum.

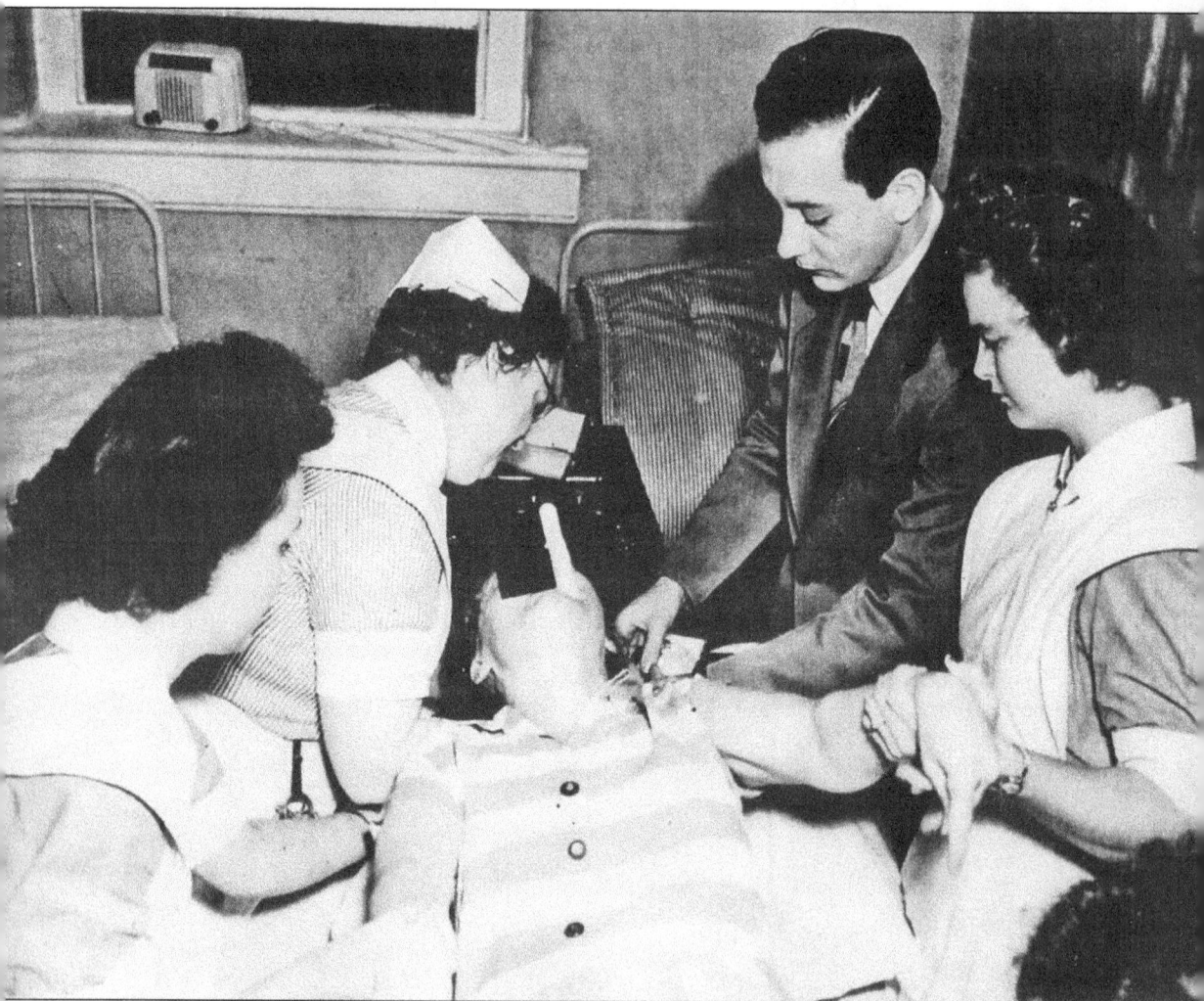

SHOCK THERAPY. This photograph of a patient being prepared for electro-convulsive therapy (ECT) was probably taken in the Foster-Wade Building around 1940. ECT involves the use of an electric current to cause the controlled induction of a seizure. This treatment has been shown to be effective for certain mental illnesses, such as major depression, and is still in use today throughout the country. An antique ECT machine from the period is included in the Spring Grove Alumni Museum's collection.

Four

RECONFIGURATION AND MODERNIZATION 1942–1980

By the end of the Great Depression, several of Spring Grove's buildings were showing the results of age and years of postponed maintenance. Shortages of labor and materials during World War I, coupled with the increasing demand for beds, further taxed the ability of the hospital to provide quality patient care. A series of newspaper articles in 1949 spotlighted the degree to which conditions in Maryland's state hospitals had deteriorated. The state's leaders were already aware of the pressing need for substantial improvements and had previously appropriated an additional $25 million to upgrade the hospitals. A flurry of new construction followed at Spring Grove over the next 20 years. However, unlike in previous eras, the new construction was largely intended to replace older, outdated buildings, rather than just to expand the capacity of the hospital.

During World War II and the following decade, Spring Grove relied on interventions such as sedative medications, talk therapy, electro-convulsive therapy, and, in some cases, psychosurgery. However, occupational therapy remained a very important treatment modality, and the farm and various industrial shops continued to be active and productive.

By the mid-1950s, following the completion of a several new buildings and the upgrading of staffing levels, conditions had improved so much that Spring Grove became one of the first five state hospitals in the country to be accredited by the Joint Commission on Accreditation of Hospitals. The first antipsychotic medication, chlorpromazine, was approved in the United States for psychiatric use in 1954 and was used at Spring Grove shortly thereafter. The hospital's census peaked at 2,807 patients in 1955 and then began to decline steadily. The shrinking census was attributable to a number of factors, including the availability of effective antipsychotic medications, better funding for community treatment and housing programs, public entitlement programs, sustained economic prosperity, and declining rates of infectious diseases.

The various research departments of the Maryland state psychiatric hospitals were combined at Spring Grove in the 1960s to form a single entity, known as the Maryland Psychiatric Research Center (MPRC). Today MPRC at Spring Grove is a leading academic center that studies the causes, manifestations, and innovative treatments of schizophrenia. During this time, the hospital's academic affiliation with the University of Maryland was strengthened.

THE WHITE BUILDING NEARING COMPLETION IN 1952. While still under construction, the building was referred to as the Disturbed Patients Building. At the time it opened, it was called the Disturbed Women's Building. It was later renamed the White Building. The building had four wards, each of which held 25 beds. It is currently used as an acute admissions building.

THE HAMILTON BUILDING UNDER CONSTRUCTION, 1952. Known originally as the Admissions Building, the six-ward, 120-bed structure was designed for the reception and treatment of newly admitted, acutely ill patients.

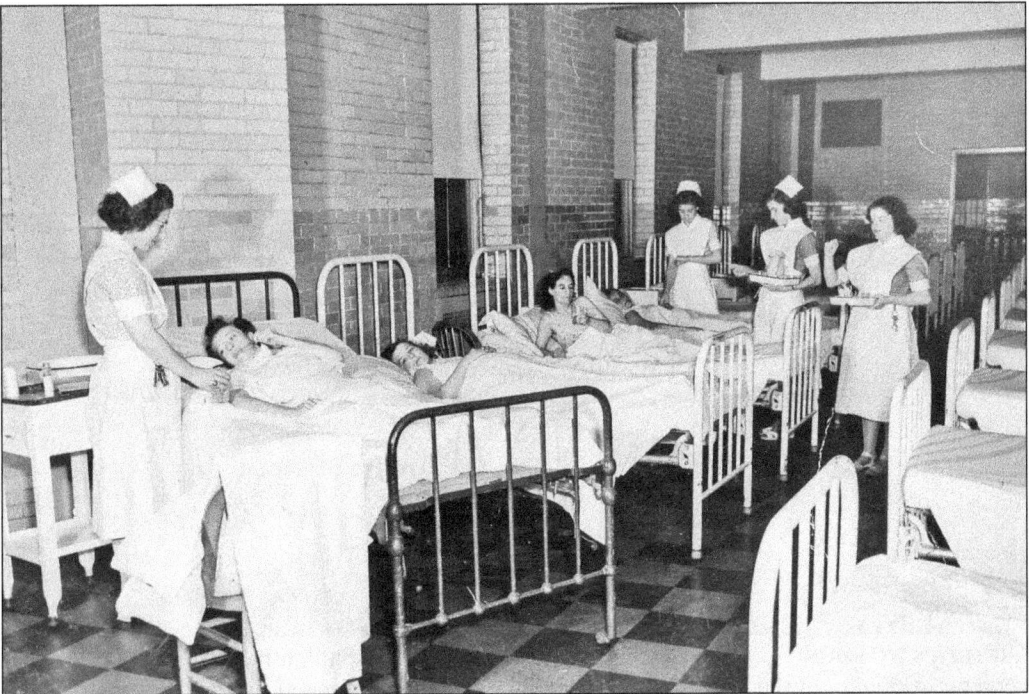

MEDICAL WARD IN THE GARRETT BUILDING, 1940S. For many years, the Garrett Building served as Spring Grove's medical-surgical building. Psychiatric patients who were also suffering from physical illnesses that required special treatment or isolation were generally treated in this building.

MAIN BUILDING. This unsigned watercolor was painted by a patient, probably in the 1950s. The original is currently hanging in the Spring Grove Alumni Museum in the Garrett Building on the grounds of Spring Grove.

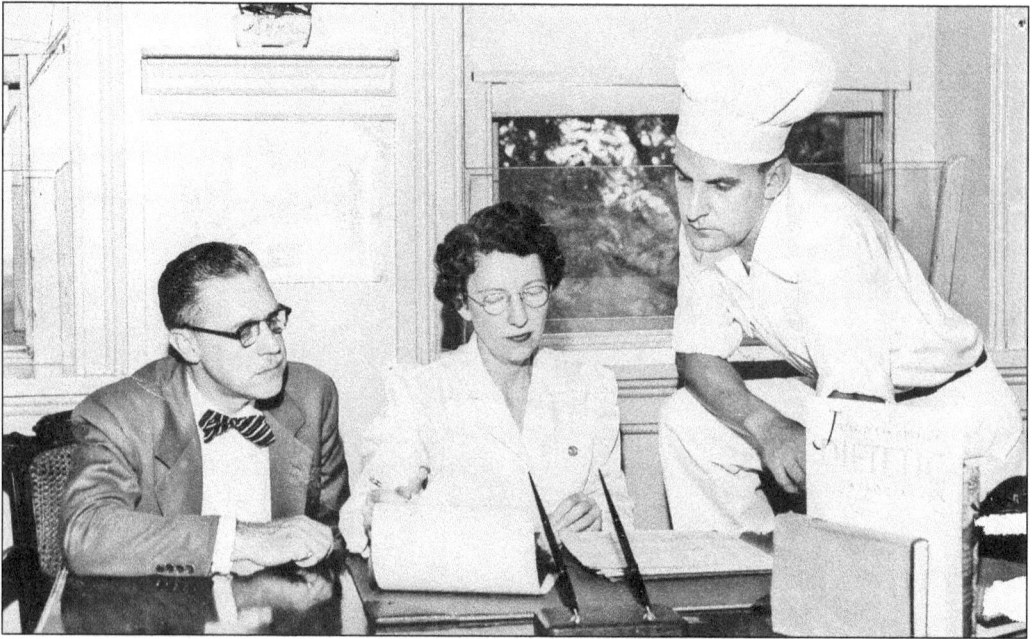

DIETETICS AT SPRING GROVE. Since the early days of the hospital, it has been recognized that good nutrition is essential to good physical and mental health. Francis Gibson, the woman seated in the center of the image, was the director of the dietetics department for many years. This photograph was taken in one of the offices in the Main Building, probably in the 1950s.

NURSES' TRAINING CLASS IN THE RICE AUDITORIUM, 1940s. The nurses seen here were evidently being given a lecture in human anatomy. Instructors at the hospital's school of practical nursing included senior nurses, members of the Spring Grove medical staff, and others. The Rice Auditorium is still used today for staff and patient education, as well as for patient activities and amusements.

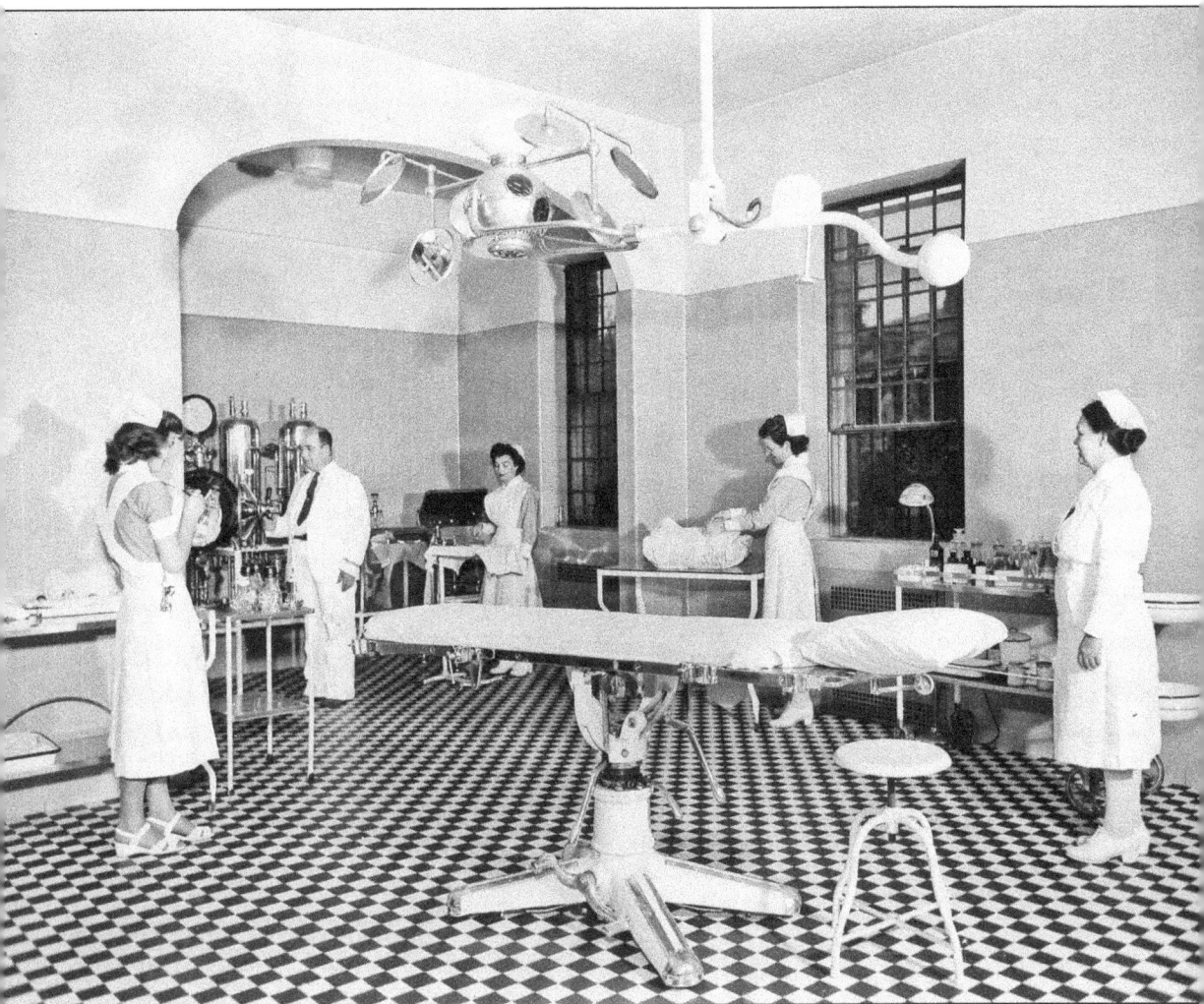

OPERATING ROOM, GARRETT BUILDING, 1940S. Until relatively recently, most routine operations required by Spring Grove's patients were performed on-site at Spring Grove by the hospital's physicians and nurses. Beginning in 1932 and continuing until the completion of the Smith Building in 1975, the Garrett Building served as the hospital's medical-surgical building. From left to right are unidentified, George Grothe, Ada Chandler, Ruth Barnes, and Nettie Lord.

EMPLOYEE VILLAGE IN THE 1940S. The cafeteria building and 12 employee cottages (above) were built in 1942, at a combined cost of $265,000, in response to the war-related housing shortage. Each of the cottages had eight double-occupancy bedrooms. There was also a full bath and a half-bath on each floor, but no kitchen, dining room, or living room. Employees and their families took their meals in the employees' cafeteria and socialized in the recreation center, which was located in the cafeteria building's basement. Nine additional employee cottages (below) were built to the south of the cafeteria building in 1948 but are no longer extant. The 1942 cottages are still in use as employee housing. A red-brick apartment building (not shown) with 20 units was added to the Employee Village in 1951, and a nurse's dormitory building (the left side of today's Tuerk Building) was opened in 1954. The Tuerk Building now provides classrooms for patient and staff education.

THE WELTMER BOWL, AS IT APPEARED IN 1949. Above, the towers of the Main Building can be seen atop the small hill in the center background. The Bland-Bryant Building is on the left and the bandstand (gazebo) is seen on the right. Below, the ball field, officially known as the Weltmer Bowl, was built between 1936 and 1945, entirely through the labor of the patients of the Bland-Bryant Building.

GRADUATES OF SPRING GROVE'S NURSE TRAINING PROGRAM, 1954. These five individuals are seen standing in front of the stage of the Rice Auditorium. The patches on their shoulders include the seal of the state of Maryland and the initials "SGSH" for "Spring Grove State Hospital." From left to right are Lorraine Green, Margaret Saylor Winstead, Imogene Clay, Catherine Barnhart Orr, and Ronnie Kitts.

AERIAL VIEW, 1952. The Stone Cottage Complex is seen at the far right in this image. The Hamilton Building, seen in the upper left quadrant, was still under construction. The Employee Village is seen at the far left, and at the center of the photograph are the Main, Foster-Wade, Garrett, and Bland-Bryant Buildings.

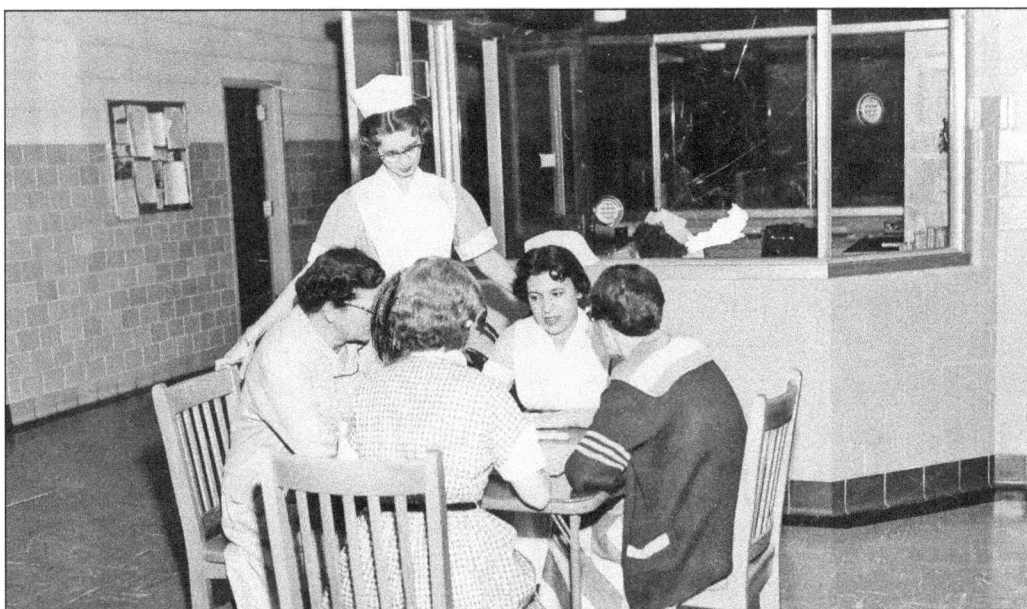

A Group of Nurses and Patients in the Hamilton Building. The 120-bed Hamilton Building opened in 1953 and originally served as Spring Grove's admissions building. It appears that the women shown in this photograph were playing Scrabble.

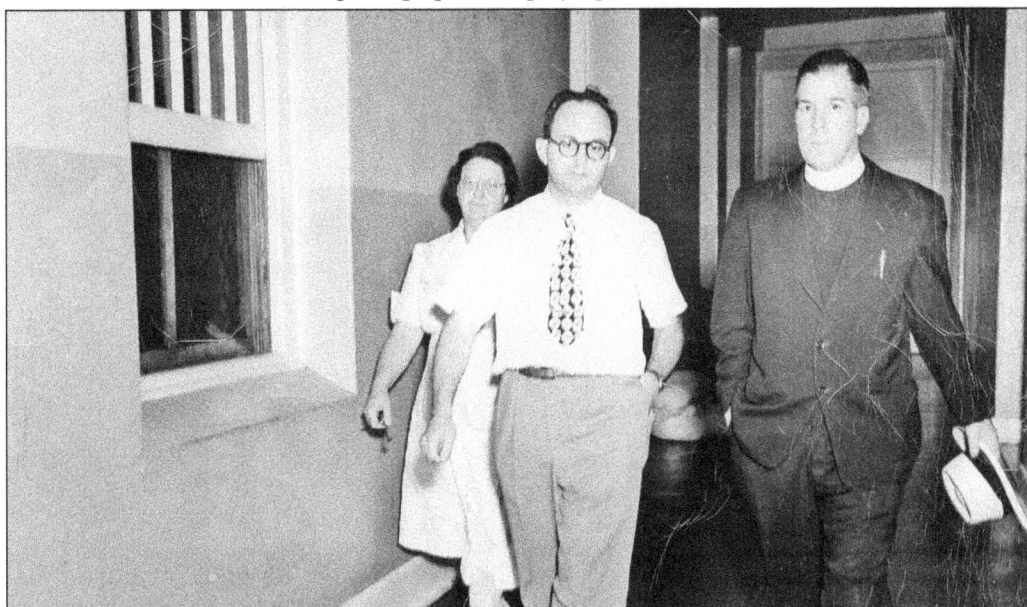

A Nurse, a Psychiatrist, and a Priest in a Corridor of the Foster-Wade Building, 1955. The subjects of this photograph are identified as Hattie Plunkert, Dr. Albert Kurland, and Father Farrell. All three individuals were members of the Spring Grove staff for many years. As her image in this photograph might suggest, Plunkert was frequently described by those who knew her as a "no-nonsense type of person." She was a 1931 graduate of the Spring Grove State Hospital Nurses Training Program, and by all accounts, Plunkert was highly dedicated to the hospital and to its patients. Dr. Kurland was actively involved in conducting research into the causes and treatments for mental illnesses.

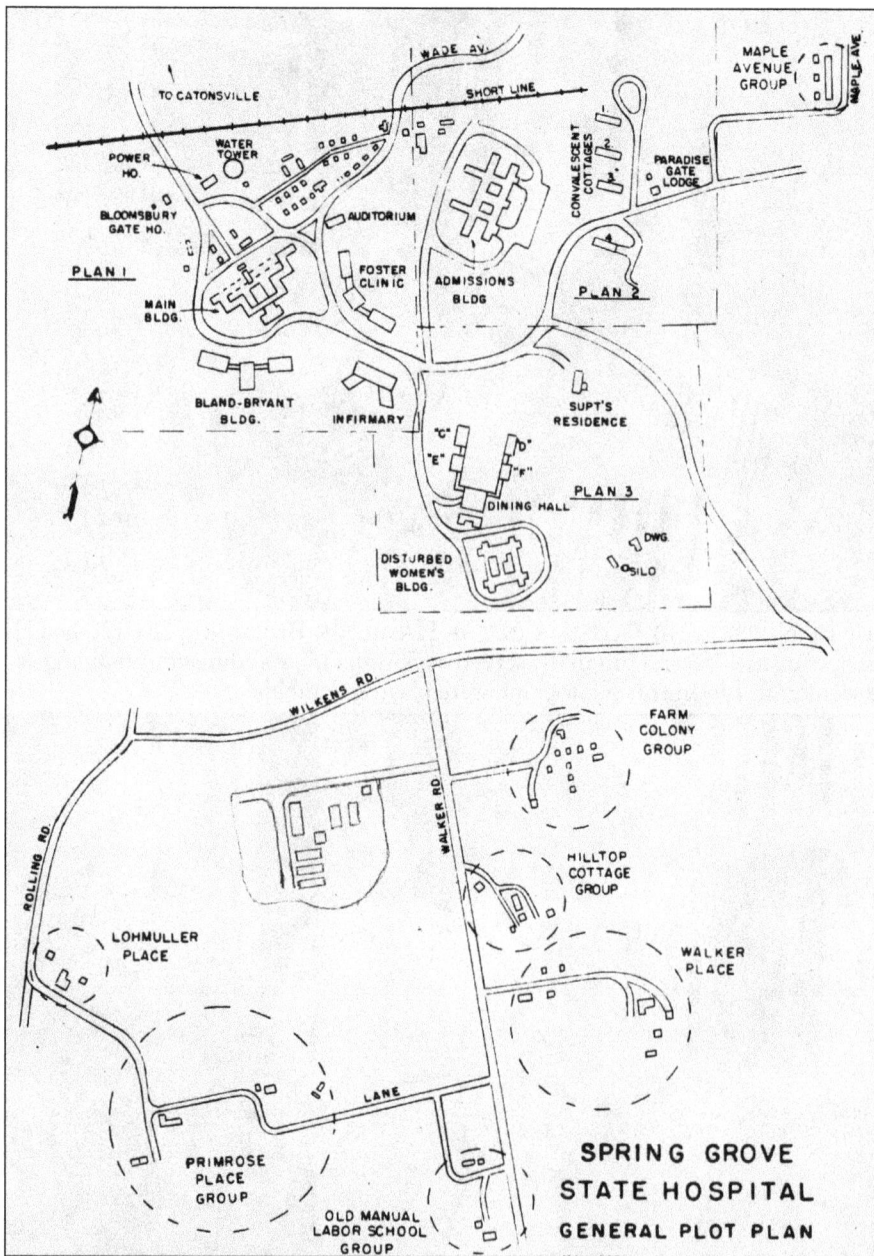

PLOT PLAN, SPRING GROVE STATE HOSPITAL, 1953. Although there are certain inaccuracies of scale, this plan shows the relative location of the major buildings and building groupings at Spring Grove State Hospital at what might be considered its peak, in terms of its size. Most of the patient care buildings were located at the northern end of the property, an area that is still occupied by the hospital today (the top half of the above image). The southern portion of the grounds was largely devoted to employee housing, horticulture, and animal husbandry—although certain buildings in this part of the property, most notably the Hillcrest Building, quartered patients. The portion of the Spring Grove State Hospital property that was south of Wilkens Avenue, approximately 430 acres, now comprises a large majority of the campus of the University of Maryland, Baltimore County (UMBC).

RED BRICK COTTAGE EXTERIOR. This photograph of one of the four Red Brick Cottages was taken shortly after the buildings were completed in 1954. Originally called "Convalescent Cottages," the buildings that are now known as the Red Brick Cottages serve those patients who tend to require longer lengths of stay in the hospital.

SPRING GROVE PHARMACY, 1953. Here Eva Barthel, a volunteer assistant in the Spring Grove pharmacy, is seen carefully measuring and weighing a chemical compound in the days in which drugs were still sometimes made in the pharmacy by combining various ingredients and forming pills and powders. Note the mortar and pestle in Barthel's left hand.

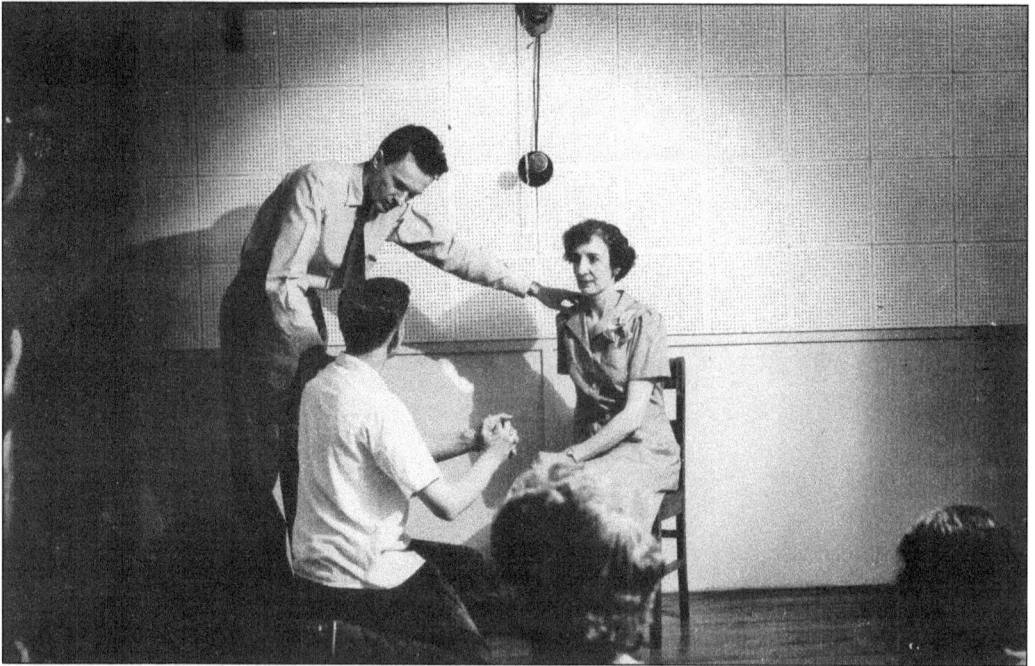

PSYCHODRAMA IN 1954. This presumably posed shot demonstrates psychodrama, a therapeutic technique in which people are encouraged to explore their feelings and problems through role-playing in a controlled and supportive environment under the guidance of a trained psychodrama therapist.

ROSE GARDEN. This photograph shows the dedication of a rose garden located in front of Stone Cottage C. Although undated, it was probably taken sometime around 1960. The man shown holding the shovel is believed to have been Maryland governor J. Millard Tawes.

MAIN BUILDING, REAR. The photographer was standing just south of the Employees' Cafeteria Building when this picture was taken sometime in the early 1960s.

MAIN BUILDING, NORTH WING, C. 1962. Persons familiar with the Spring Grove campus today will recognize the parking lot at the right in this photograph as the parking lot that is currently directly in front of the Jamison Building. The Main Building was demolished in early 1964, and today the site of its north wing is occupied by the c. 1981 Jamison patient canteen and activity building.

DAYHOFF BUILDING, C. 1961. The three men shown standing at the front entrance of the Dayhoff Building are, from left to right, Dr. Bruno Radauskus, Everett Dayhoff, and Dr. Isadore Tuerk. Dr. Radauskus was the current superintendent; Dr. Tuerk was the superintendent who had immediately preceded him; and Dayhoff, after whom the building was named, had been a highly regarded longtime member of the hospital's administration. The Dayhoff Building was dedicated in 1961 and was originally known as the Active Treatment Building for Men. Today it is one of the hospital's two acute admissions buildings. Persons who knew Everett Dayhoff referred to him as a jack of all trades. He coached the hospital's highly successful baseball teams during the 1940s and held various titles, including "Director of Amusements." A veteran of World War I, Dayhoff received training as a medic in the army and served as the director of bandaging for the Spring Grove practical nursing school.

SAMUEL WARREN HAMILTON, M.D. Dr. Hamilton, after whom the Hamilton Building at Spring Grove was named, was a member of the U.S. Public Health Service and a president of the American Psychiatric Association. In 1939, he published a report that helped lead to the development of a list of hospital standards that were approved by the APA in 1946.

THE MAIN BUILDING IN ITS FINAL YEARS. Although this picture is undated, the presence of two 1960 Fords indicates that it was taken sometime during the last several years of the building's existence. The main building was razed in 1964.

LOBBY OF THE MAIN BUILDING. This is the only known photograph that shows the lobby of the Main Building. Note the mosaic tile floor that reads, "Founded 1797." When the Main Building was demolished, this section of the tile floor was preserved and is currently on display in Spring Grove's museum in the Garrett Building.

WOMAN LOOKING OUT A WINDOW OF THE GARRETT BUILDING. This rather haunting image was the cover of the Spring Grove patient handbook in 1959.

MAIN BUILDING DEMOLITION BEGINS. The 110-year-old Main Building was torn down in 1964 after it was found to be structurally unsound and beyond repair. Ricky Sanphilipo, one of the men who assisted in the demolition of the building, recently told the authors that the grand old building did not give up the ghost gracefully. Some of the interior bearing walls were reportedly as many as 13 courses of brick thick, and demolition took considerably longer than had been anticipated.

ADOLESCENT UNIT, MID-1960S. The Moylan Building was built in 1965 to house Spring Grove's child and adolescent wards. The woman seen at the doorway was Augusta Farley, a longtime volunteer at Spring Grove State Hospital.

SPRING GROVE'S CHILDREN PATIENTS SEE FORT MCHENRY WITH THE MARINES, 1959. Children had been admitted to the hospital at least as early as the 1840s. For example, the census on December 31, 1849, included three patients under the age of 15, along with an additional four patients between 15 and 20 years old. The medical superintendent's report of 1879 notes that a nine-year-old boy had been admitted to Spring Grove on the basis of a court order, and in 1896, six adolescents were admitted, two of whom were under the age of 15. (Modern parents may find it interesting to note that "puberty" was listed as the "alleged cause of insanity" in a number of the adolescent cases in the 19th century.)

PATIENT CANTEEN, FOSTER-WADE BUILDING, 1954. The patient canteens have traditionally offered snacks and refreshments, such hot dogs, candy, packaged cakes, and soft drinks. Also offered were toys, costume jewelry, scarves, clocks, wallets, cigarettes, cosmetics, and toiletries.

CHAPEL, LOWER LEVEL, RICE AUDITORIUM. This undated photograph, probably taken in the late 1950s or early 1960s, shows a chapel that was once located in the basement of the Rice Auditorium Building. The space was originally used an occupational therapy shop when the building first opened, in the mid-1930s. (Courtesy of Catonsville Room, Catonsville Public Library.)

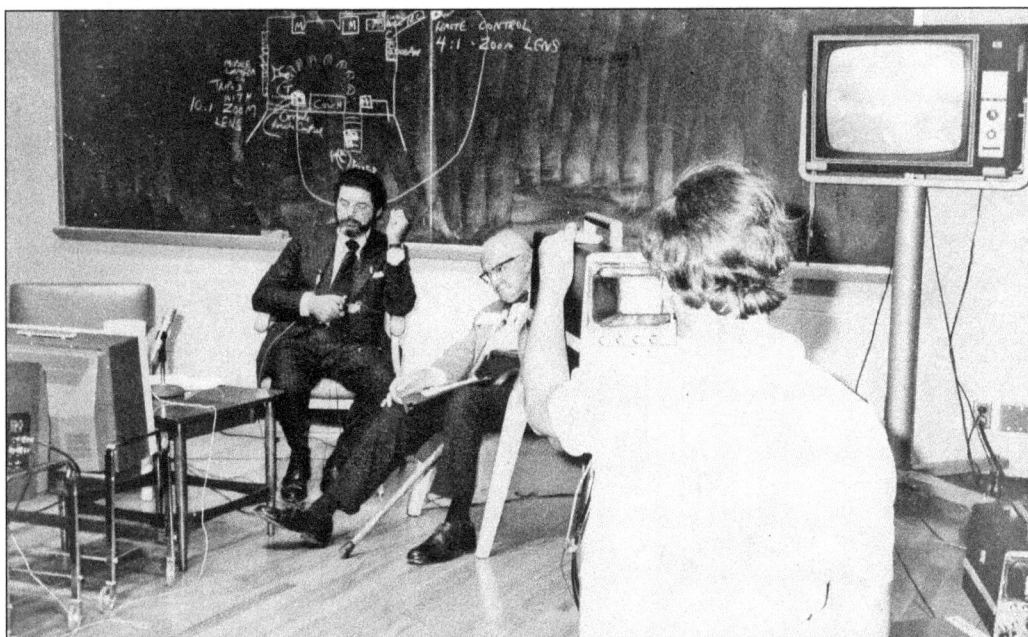

EDUCATIONAL SERVICES. For a number of years, Spring Grove's closed-circuit television network was used to broadcast live and videotaped educational programs to staff and patients throughout the hospital. Spring Grove continues to serve as a popular training site for students in professional training in a number of health-related fields.

OPENING OF THE NEW WING OF THE TUERK BUILDING, 1976. Today's Tuerk Building was originally called the Nurses Home and was built in 1954 as a dormitory for the nursing staff. In 1976, the size of the building more than doubled when a second wing was added on the east side. Seen here from left to right are Ann Stevens, Helen Tuerk, and Dr. Isadore Tuerk. Stevens was an administrative assistant to the superintendent for a number of years beginning in the 1930s. She was highly instrumental in the establishment of the Spring Grove Alumni Museum in 1997 and still plays a guiding role as a consultant to Spring Grove's Museum Committee.

SPRING GROVE EMPLOYEE BAND AT THE DEDICATION OF THE TUERK BUILDING, APRIL 7, 1976. The newly completed east wing of the Tuerk Building can be seen in the right background. The band was known as P. J. and the Guys. From left to right are Peggy Johnson, Fenou Davis, Lamont Williams, Samuel Dow, Ken Morrison, and Ronnel Dow.

PATIENTS AND STAFF ATTEND THE JAMISON PATIENT CANTEEN BUILDING GRAND OPENING. The Jamison Building was built in 1980 through funds that were donated to the hospital by a grateful family of a former patient. It was dedicated in 1981.

Five

DAILY LIFE AT SPRING GROVE

The Spring Grove of yesterday was in many ways a self-contained socialist community—both for patients and for staff. Although many patients stayed only a short time, other patients lived out their lives at the hospital. Staff members typically resided in housing that was provided by the hospital, and many raised their families at Spring Grove. Medical care was provided to patients and staff alike by the hospital's physicians and nurses. Both patients and staff took advantage of amusements such as the concerts, dances, and, later on, movies that were offered on-site. The grounds included tennis courts for many years. Golf links were added in the 1890s and were used by patients and staff. Also in the early days, there were horse-drawn carriages that were maintained to give patients rides in countryside. Most patients occupied themselves during the day with work—either on the farm, on the wards, or in one of a number of industrial shops. Employees shared meals in the employee dining rooms and socialized after hours in various staff lounges. There was a patient-staff orchestra, a patient glee club, and, at the beginning of the 20th century, a newspaper that was written and printed by patients.

LAWN IN FRONT OF THE MAIN BUILDING. The carriage porch of the Main Building can be faintly distinguished to the right of the large tree in the center of the image.

VIEW OF THE SPRING GROVE STATE HOSPITAL GROUNDS. The photographer was standing just south of the location of the Bland-Bryant Building and was looking across the lawn toward the Main Building, which can be faintly distinguished between the trees.

AMUSEMENT HALL IN 1899. A passage in the hospital's annual report of 1877 reads, "The large room in the rear of the center building, on the second floor, has been fitted up as a place of amusement, where the tedium of many idle hours is beguiled in dances, concerts, musicals, etc. These amusements do good service in diverting the mind from its morbid fancies and by directing it into healthier channels." The space was also used for Catholic and Protestant worship services.

A SCENE ON THE GROUNDS. While indoor amusements were available around the year, both formal and informal activities were also available on the grounds, weather permitting. Today, as always, patients and staff gather strength and pleasure from the peaceful beauty of the hospital's open spaces.

PATIENT REFECTORY, 1899, MAIN BUILDING. There were separate refectories for males and females in the center section of the Main Building. Patients who weren't able to leave their wards to go to the refectories were served meals on their wards.

MAIN BUILDING KITCHEN, DATE UNKNOWN. The building's central kitchen was located on the first floor, at the back of the center section. Prepared food was then delivered to each of the dining rooms on the upper floors through a series of manually operated dumbwaiters. (See Main Building Floor Plan, page 23.)

BILLIARDS IN A DAY ROOM IN THE FOSTER CLINIC, C. 1920. Originally called the Psychopathic Building, the imposing structure that was to become known as the Foster-Wade Building was designed to serve as Spring Grove's admissions, acute care, and medical treatment building. The cornerstone of the building was laid in 1914, but the building didn't actually open until July 1920. For its first five years, the Foster Clinic cared for World War I veterans who were suffering from psychiatric illnesses. The building took on a purely civilian role in the second half of the 1920s when most of the remaining veterans were transferred to the newly built Perry Point Veteran's Hospital in northeastern Maryland.

SPRING GROVE BASEBALL TEAM. Although the men's uniforms say "Catonsville," the players were from Spring Grove. In the 1920s, Spring Grove had a baseball team that included both patients and employees.

SPRING GROVE BASEBALL TEAM, 1920s. In the 1920s, Spring Grove's patient-staff baseball teams played against local college teams—and often won.

SPRING GROVE STATE HOSPITAL BASEBALL CLUB, 1946. The man seated in the first row, second from the left, is Everett Dayhoff, the man in whose honor the Dayhoff Building at Spring Grove is named. The patches on the shoulders of the men's uniforms read: "M.A.B.A. 1943 Champs." M.A.B.A. stands for Maryland Amateur Baseball Association.

THE BANDSTAND, C. 1944. This structure is known today as the gazebo, but it was originally called the bandstand. Built on a slope above the athletic field, the lower level held locker rooms for the players.

BAKESHOP EXTERIOR, 1922. This building was constructed to serve as a bakeshop and was used to make bread and other baked goods for many years. Today it is used as the hospital's paint shop.

SPRING GROVE BAKESHOP INTERIOR. These men are in the process of preparing loaves of bread for baking. Note the large dough mixing machine along the rear wall and the rows of bread pans in the foreground.

SPRING GROVE COOK, 1940S. The man shown dishing up a plate of food in front of the vintage coal stove has been identified as Jeffrey Olsten Lester, a Spring Grove State Hospital cook. The location of the photograph is the bakeshop, which was also known as the Cook Shop. Several family members of Lester's generation worked for the hospital, and currently his daughter, Pat Massey, is a supervisor in the Spring Grove Health Information Services Department.

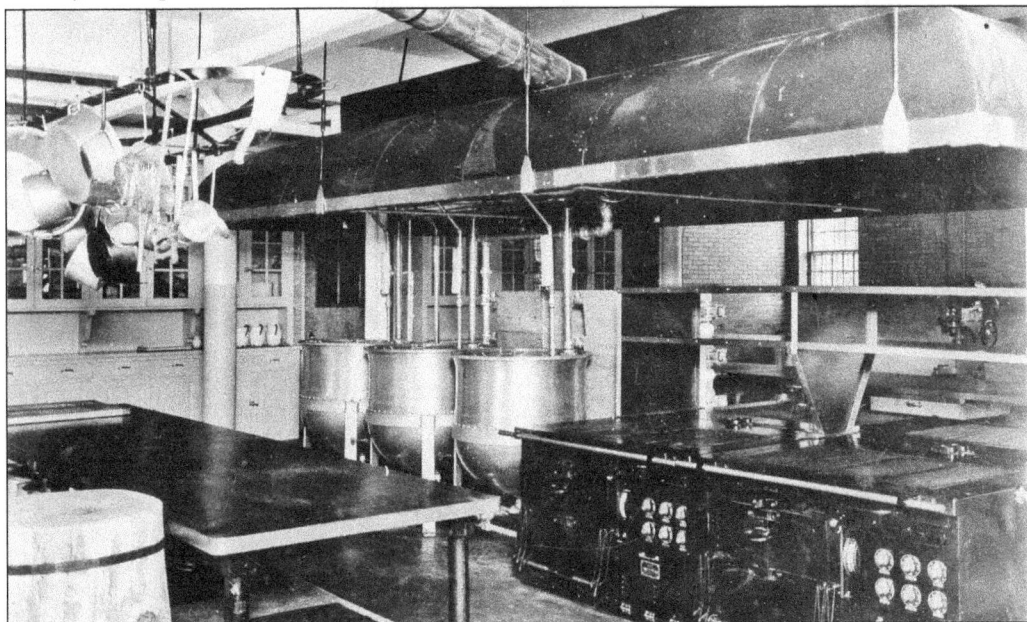

GARRETT BUILDING KITCHEN. This undated photograph of the Garrett Building's kitchen was probably taken around 1934, when the Garrett Building opened. For many years, each of the larger patient care buildings or building groupings at Spring Grove had its own separate kitchen and cook staff. Today the space shown in this photograph has been extensively remodeled and is occupied by the Spring Grove pharmacy.

PATIENT DINING ROOM, FOSTER-WADE BUILDING. This undated photograph of a patient dining room was taken in the Foster-Wade Building. Prepared food was delivered from the basement kitchen to service pantries on the wards via a series of dumbwaiters.

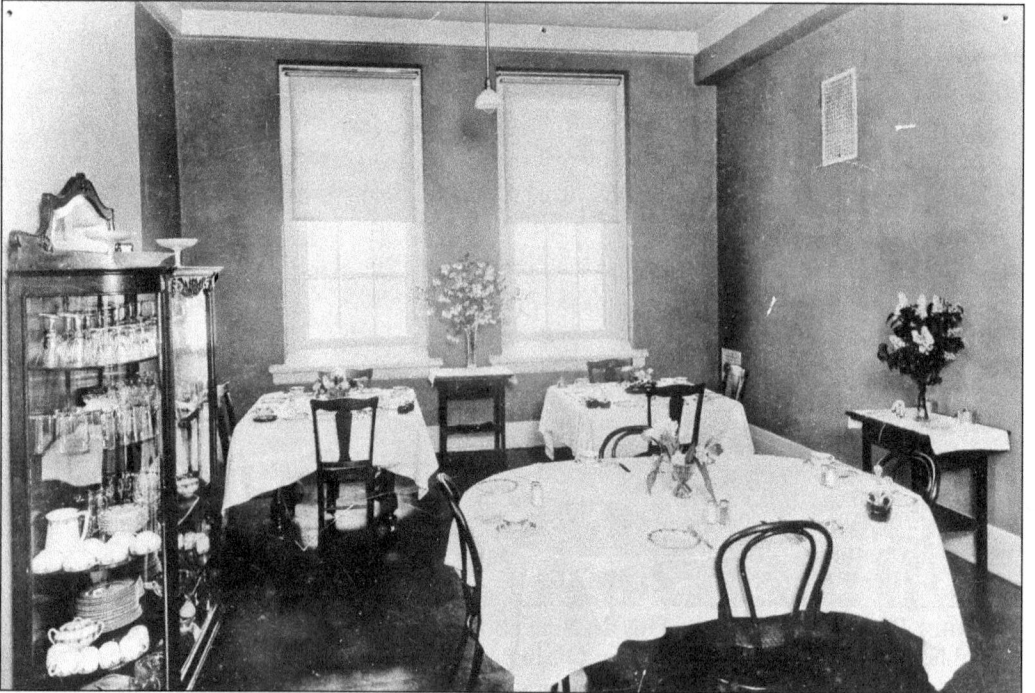

FOSTER-WADE BUILDING, STAFF DINING ROOM, C. 1930. The flowers on the tables almost certainly would have been grown on the grounds of the hospital or in one of its greenhouses.

GARRETT BUILDING PATIENT DINING ROOM. The Spring Grove pharmacy now occupies most of the first two floors of the Garrett Building. In addition, the building houses the hospital's museum.

CAFETERIA, HAMILTON BUILDING, 1950S. Some of the elements shown in this picture, such as the stainless-steel tray line, were installed in the employees' cafeteria (now known as the Café on the Grove) when it was remodeled in 2005.

SPRING GROVE ORCHESTRA, RICE AUDITORIUM, 1938. The picture's original caption reads as follows: "The Beacon of 1938 has the pleasure to announce that after a number of years, Spring Grove again has a concert and dance orchestra. Under the experienced direction of Mr. Joseph Tiszl, the whole-hearted support of Dr. Silas Weltmer, and the cooperation of others of the hospital staff, the orchestra which at first seemed only a far-fetched dream became a pleasant enjoyable reality. The original aim of having as many patients as possible play in the orchestra has been attained since they make up the majority of the members. It is a very general opinion that the orchestra, in the few months it has been organized, probably equals and excells [sic] any hospital orchestra in the country." (The *Beacon* was the yearbook of the Spring Grove Nursing School.)

LAWN CONCERT GIVEN BY THE SPRING GROVE ORCHESTRA. In the 1930s and 1940s, Spring Grove's patient-staff orchestra often performed at picnics and other outdoor events.

MAIN DINING ROOM OF THE EMPLOYEES' CAFETERIA, C. 1942. The Employees' Cafeteria Building was built in 1942 in order to provide a central employee dining facility. The cafeteria offered three meals a day, six days a week. The prices, which were subsidized by the hospital, were quite low. For example, in 1953, a shrimp salad sandwich cost 15¢ and a full breakfast that included eggs, toast, bacon, and coffee cost just 20¢. Of course, these prices must be considered within the context of similarly low salaries. The starting salary for a male attendant at Spring Grove in the early 1950s was around $40 per week.

CAFÉ ON THE GROVE, TODAY. This picture shows the Employees' Cafeteria Building as it appears today. This photograph and the one above it were taken from the same position, approximately 63 years apart.

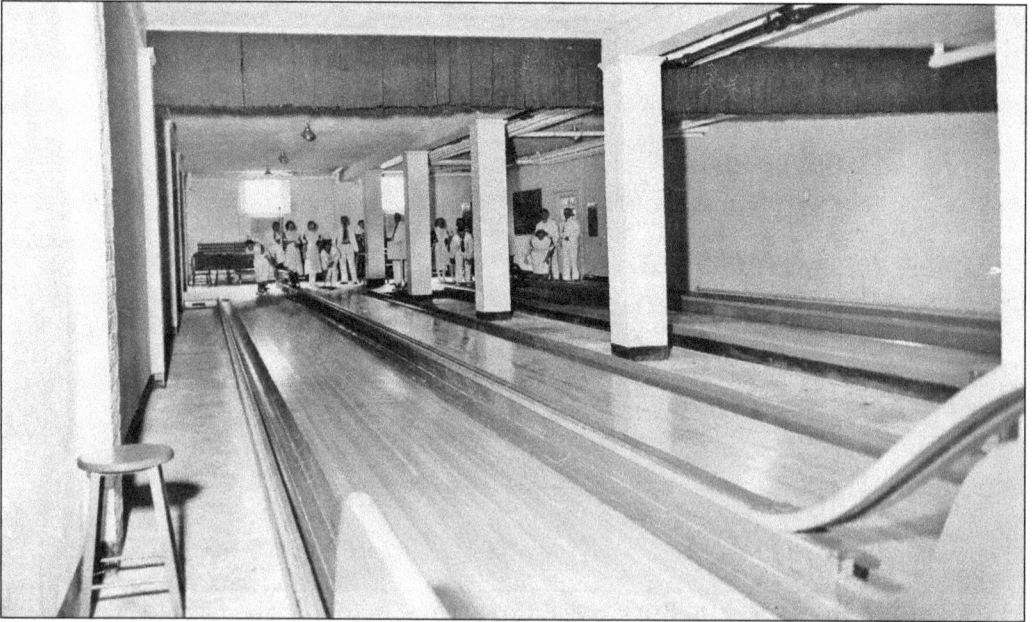

BOWLING ALLEYS IN THE EMPLOYEES' CAFETERIA. The lower level of the c. 1942 Employees' Cafeteria Building once housed an employee recreation center that included a four-lane bowling alley. The records indicate that the hospital had bowling alleys, in various locations, dating back to the 1880s.

STAFF RECREATION CENTER, EMPLOYEES' CAFETERIA BASEMENT, EARLY 1940s. In addition to the bowling alleys shown above, the recreation center offered table tennis, billiards, chess, checkers, and cards, as well as a reading room and a writing room. There was also a snack bar that served soft drinks and various types of sandwiches. Later on, one of the first television sets at Spring Grove was installed here.

OPENING OF A PATIENT CANTEEN, NOVEMBER 1952. Sponsored by the Women's Auxiliary of Spring Grove State Hospital, the canteen operated in this location for several years. The man seen standing at the counter, in the center, was Clifton T. Perkins, M.D., after whom one of Maryland's other state hospitals is named. The Patient Canteen was relocated to Foster-Wade Building in 1954 and to the Jamison Building in 1981.

CANTEEN SERVICE FOR THE HILLCREST BUILDING, 1954. Because the patients who were confined to the maximum security Hillcrest Building were generally not permitted to leave the building to go to the central Patient Canteen, it was necessary to provide those patients with special delivery services. Note that although the volunteer is seen holding bars of soap in her left hand, the basket appears to be entirely filled with cartons of cigarettes.

CHRISTMAS PARTY AT THE SUPERINTENDENT'S HOUSE 1954. The man seen standing at the far left of the picture was Isadore Tuerk, M.D., superintendent of Spring Grove. This photograph was taken in the living room of the Superintendent's House.

THE SUPERINTENDENT'S HOUSE. The stately Georgian revival brick home was built in 1940 on the grounds of Spring Grove as a dwelling for the superintendent and the superintendent's family.

ONE OF THE SPRING-FED PONDS AT SPRING GROVE. As its name would suggest, Spring Grove is dotted with spring-fed rivulets and small ponds. Originally the springs served both as the source of freshwater and, downstream, as the terminus of the hospital's sewer pipes. A septic system was built after a court order in the 1880s prevented the hospital from continuing to dump sewage into its streams.

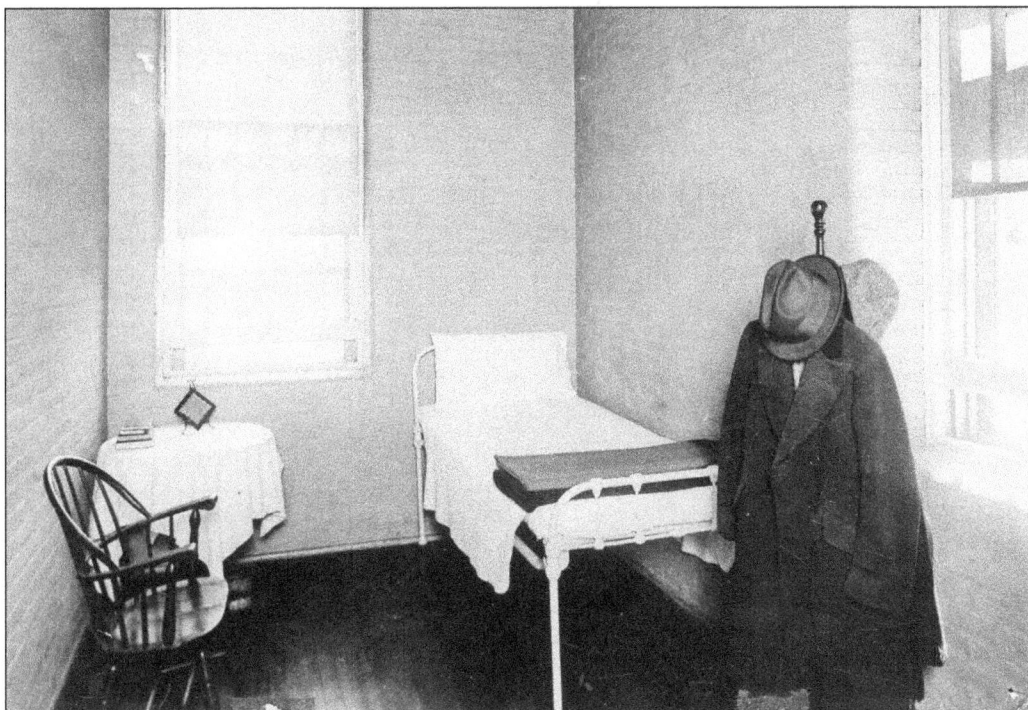

PATIENT BEDROOM, GARRETT BUILDING C WARD. This photograph shows a private bedroom that was used to isolate patients who had infectious diseases.

RULES
OF
MARYLAND HOSPITAL.

1. Each Attendant shall be dressed and ready for duty in the morning at 5 o'clock in the summer, and 7 o'clock in the winter, unless excused or sick.

2. The Attendants shall have their wards ready for inspection by 10 o'clock.

3. The airing courts shall also be kept clean by the Attendants.

4. The Attendants must see that their patients are washed, properly dressed, and ready for their meals at the proper hours. Absence from any meal to be reported to the Supervisor.

5. Attendants must not confine patients to their rooms without direction of one of the Physicians, and every such confinement shall be reported in Supervisor's daily report.

6. No restraining apparatus of any kind must be used, without the express direction of one of the Physicians. Such use to be always mentioned in daily report of Supervisor.

7. Attendants will maintain order in their wards, without undue physical force, or overbearing conduct. They will, by kindness and attention to the wants of the patients, better acquire their respect and confidence, so that their wishes and efforts for order will be respected. Disorderly or excited conduct of any patient should be reported at once to the Physician or Supervisor.

8. All irritating language or conduct on the part of Attendants is strictly forbidden to be used towards patients, nor will any threats or means of punishment be permitted.

9. Profanity, swearing or vulgar conversation is strictly forbidden on the part of all Attendants and others employed in the Institution. Any blow, kick or violence to a patient, will subject the perpetrator to loss of his situation.

10. Every patient, unless otherwise directed, will be bathed once a week. In bathing, care should be taken that the self respect of the patient is not wounded, but that everything be done for his comfort — that the water be of proper temperature, and that towels and other conveniences be provided. In no case must the head be placed or kept under water.

11. No visitors will be taken into the wards or allowed to remain there without the permission of the Medical Superintendent or the assistant Physician.

12. All wrong-doing — violation of these rules, or any improper conduct, should be reported by any Officer, Attendant, or Employee of the Hospital to the Medical Superintendent.

Henry S. Taylor
President

RULES OF THE MARYLAND HOSPITAL, C. 1880. Staff members of today's Spring Grove Hospital Center are amused by the comparison between the brevity of the above one-page document and the hospital's current multi-volume policy and procedure manuals. However, the basic principles that are reflected in the 1880 rules remain unchanged. The document is signed by Col. Henry S. Taylor, who was president of the board of managers for the Maryland Hospital for the Insane at Spring Grove in 1880.

Six

THE TRADITION CONTINUES

Today's Spring Grove Hospital Center is a busy and vital place that continues to build on its more-than-two-century traditions of compassionate care and enlightened treatment of mental illnesses. Today's Spring Grove operates 440 beds and is Maryland's largest psychiatric hospital. Several thousand individuals receive treatment on the campus each year.

The hospital maintains major teaching affiliations with the University of Maryland, as well as with a number of other institutions of higher education. Training opportunities exist for medical students, psychiatric residents and fellows, psychology interns and externs, master's-level clinical social work students, nurses, nursing assistants, and others. Spring Grove is also the host site of the Maryland Psychiatric Research Center, a leading research institution that enjoys an international reputation for excellence.

Just as their 19th- and 20th-century predecessors, today's patients and residents are able to take advantage of the hospital's scenic setting, its quiet, park-like campus, its privacy, and the benefits of the skilled care and treatment that are provided here.

Spring Grove always has been and always will be an asylum, in the very best sense of the word: a place of refuge, compassionate care, assistance, and healing.

SPRING GROVE CAMPUS TODAY. The building seen in the center background is the Maryland Psychiatric Research Center's headquarters building. The structure's official name (rarely used today) is the Spiro T. Agnew Building.

THREE OF SPRING GROVE'S HISTORIC BUILDINGS AS THEY APPEAR TODAY. At left is the original *c.* 1853 boiler house (now used as the hospital's laundry). The original boiler house is all that remains of the Main Building complex. The building in the right foreground is the 1872 firehouse, and the building with the tall smokestack in the background in the 1932 powerhouse.

THE SMITH BUILDING AND THE GAZEBO. The Smith Building serves as the hospital's current medical building and infirmary. The 1944 gazebo still stands in its original location and is often used as a quiet place in which to sit and reflect.

MEDICAL STAFF, SPRING GROVE'S BICENTENNIAL YEAR. The hospital's medical staff is shown standing beside the Rice Auditorium in 1997.

SPRING GROVE MEDICAL STAFF EXECUTIVE COMMITTEE, 1997. From left to right are Mark Pecevich, M.D.; Ronald Gray, M.D.; David Helsel, M.D., (coauthor); Rochelle Herman, M.D.; Kripa Kashyap, M.D.; and David Herman, M.D.

EMPLOYEES ENJOYING LUNCH AT THE CAFÉ ON THE GROVE. In 2005, following extensive remodeling, the hospital reopened the Employees' Cafeteria Building.

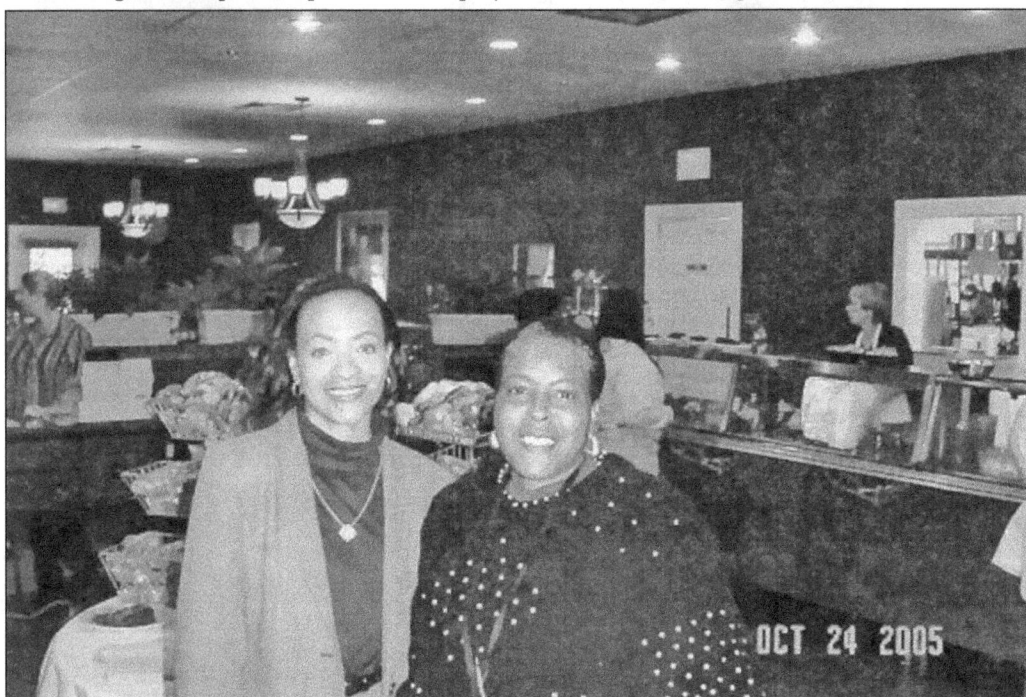

SHEILAH DAVENPORT AND GWEN JOHNSON AT THE CAFÉ ON THE GROVE. The Café on the Grove, as it is now called, is a popular dining spot that is open to all. For additional information, visit www.springgrove.com/cafe/cafe.html.

ADDING THE FINISHING TOUCHES TO A NEW SIGN AT THE VALLEY ROAD ENTRANCE. The two Spring Grove carpenters shown are Mike Thomas and Ben Edwards. Now in its third century, Spring Grove looks forward to continuing to serve Maryland with pride.

INDEX

ACROSS AMERICA, PEOPLE ARE DISCOVERING SOMETHING WONDERFUL. *THEIR HERITAGE.*

Arcadia Publishing is the leading local history publisher in the United States. With more than 4,000 titles in print and hundreds of new titles released every year, Arcadia has extensive specialized experience chronicling the history of communities and celebrating America's hidden stories, bringing to life the people, places, and events from the past. To discover the history of other communities across the nation, please visit:

www.arcadiapublishing.com

Customized search tools allow you to find regional history books about the town where you grew up, the cities where your friends and family live, the town where your parents met, or even that retirement spot you've been dreaming about.

MAP SEARCH